T0342636

THE D.I.Y. NEWSROOM

THE D.I.Y. NEWSROOM

5 STEPS TO POWERFUL AND STRATEGIC COMMUNICATIONS USING YOUR ORGANISATION'S OWN RESOURCES

STUART HOWIE

"Ready to unlock your content superpowers? Stuart articulates the skills that every storyteller needs today and the blueprint for managers to build the decentralised newsroom of tomorrow."

Yusuf Omar, co-founder Hashtag Our Story, Prince of Mojo (mobile journalism), former CNN social media storyteller

"Communication without truth and authenticity is like a house with a shaky foundation. Stuart captures the importance of checking in on truth from all angles as you develop personal or organisational strategies.

"He leaves readers with an absolute wealth of tools to effectively give and get the right information in the right way at the right time."

Elly Johnson, International Truth, Trust and Deception Authority, truthability.com

"My organisation has messages for governments, policy makers, the commentariat and my members, but it's hard to compete with the noise of others and to break through.

"This book is accessible for small organisations such as mine but has lessons for all organisations no matter the size.

"I am particularly heartened by Stuart's exhortation for content, content, content.

"Important messages are lost in entertainment value or couched as false news. These are serious times. More than ever, we must heed the straight-shooting messages in *The DIY Newsroom*."

Craig Robertson, CEO, TAFE Directors Australia

"As a newsroom manager, Stuart Howie was one of the most engaging and innovative editors in the Australian media landscape. Now that he is translating his newsroom nous to the wider corporate world, others can tap into that knowledge and reconsider how they manage their external communications.

"Whether you work in a large or small corporation, or a school, or a community organisation or sporting group – there are lessons in this book that will enable you to connect far more closely with your audience and give you the opportunity to be the editor of your own DIY Newsroom."

Paul Nolan, Director of Community Development, St Patrick's College, Ballarat

"As a storyteller and editor Stuart Howie's great skill, among many, is to distill the complex down to the points that matter, and the facts that need to be heard and understood. He makes the story simple, telling it in a manner that entertains, informs and provokes.

"In *The DIY Newsroom*, Stuart has navigated the noise and nonsense that is today's fragmented media and communication landscape, a landscape that can overwhelm even the most experienced media pro. And he presents a recipe for communication success in easy-to-understand language.

"That is why anyone with a communication need must read *The DIY Newsroom*. That it's also told in Stuart's usual entertaining way is a bonus."

Michael Stevens, Director, Print Mastheads, Fairfax Media

"*The DIY Newsroom* is a no-nonsense, easy-to-implement guide for brands daunted by the idea of producing content. Stuart provides great advice that can guide even the smallest brands to produce quality, relevant content that attracts and retains customers. Highly recommended!"

Tara Hunt, CEO, Truly Social Inc (Toronto, Canada)

Dedication

To the truth seekers and storytellers.
And to the ultimate focus group for my
communications – good, bad and indifferent:
Toni, Rory, Grace and Charlotte.

First published in 2018 by Stuart Howie

© Stuart Howie 2018
The moral rights of the author have been asserted

FLAME™
TREE
MEDIA

The DIY Newsroom™ and SMART Way™ methodology are the intellectual property of Flame Tree Media Pty Ltd, Australia

All rights reserved. Except as permitted under the *Australian Copyright Act 1968* (for example, a fair dealing for the purposes of study, research, criticism or review), no part of this book may be reproduced, stored in a retrieval system, communicated or transmitted in any form or by any means without prior written permission.

All inquiries should be made to the author.

A catalogue entry for this book is available from the National Library of Australia.

ISBN: 978-1-925648-82-9

Project management and text design by Michael Hanrahan Publishing
Cover design by Peter Reardon
Cartoons by Peter Broelman
Printed in Australia by McPherson's Printing

The paper this book is printed on is certified as environmentally friendly.

Disclaimer: The material in this publication is of the nature of general comment only, and does not represent professional advice. It is not intended to provide specific guidance for particular circumstances and it should not be relied on as the basis for any decision to take action or not take action on any matter which it covers. Readers should obtain professional advice where appropriate, before making any such decision. To the maximum extent permitted by law, the author and publisher disclaim all responsibility and liability to any person, arising directly or indirectly from any person taking or not taking action based on the information in this publication.

CONTENTS

INTRODUCTION

Do you get the feeling that with all the communication tools at our disposal that we have become too clever for our own good?

For tens of thousands of years, Australia's first people have passed on their stories effectively and powerfully with what many would regard as primitive methods: face-to-face storytelling, rock paintings, rituals, dance and message sticks.

Today, we use mobile phones to communicate instantly and we connect with people on the other side of the planet with live video. In our businesses, we engage with customers with websites and e-newsletters. We sell them stuff via online product shops. And we say whatever we want to say with an array of social media. Facebook, Twitter, LinkedIn, Pinterest, Instagram, Snapchat, WeChat. And so on. And so on.

Then there's the media formats and methods at our disposal, to build the brand of our companies and indeed ourselves. Podcasts, webinars, corporate presentations, traditional media such as print, radio and TV. Blogs, vlogs, infographics and workshops.

Never before have we had so many ways to communicate. But never has it been so complex.

We are richer, more sophisticated and more intelligent than any generation before us. The sad reality is that most of this messaging never sees the light of day – it goes off into the internet ether, lost in the cacophony of communications.

Our response? We turned communications into a field of study, as a science and high art, and elevated it to an industry. It has even become its own economy. But still, we are overwhelmed, confused and frustrated.

I have seen organisation after organisation make a meal of their communications, spending big money for little results. How many "innovative new marketing solutions" now sit in wrack and ruin on the road to nowhere? And I've seen even the best in the business self-combust from the digital disruption sweeping through society. Meantime, many comms teams are locked into the vanity game of chasing likes and shares but the result is diddly-squat sales conversions.

However, there is a better way to simple, strategic and sustainable communications: the SMART Way™, which will connect you to the people who matter the most for maximum impact.

Which is the point of this book. *The DIY Newsroom* lays out before you a simple step-by-step process that will put you out in front of your sector. This book puts method to the madness.

This is not an aspiration. It is a promise. I show you how the SMART Way has worked for big companies and small not-for-profits, and the rewards that come your way when you dare to take your light from under the bushel.

I've done the thinking for you, distilled the sheer complexity, drawn on decades of experience in traditional and new media, and provided you with the ultimate communications playbook. Yes, there's plenty here about social media, technology and modern media methods. But at the heart of what I describe are the timeless lessons about great storytelling – and how to create an audience and to hold its interest.

That's what great newsrooms do, and why they are the perfect model, pressure tested over generations.

If you are a leader in an organisation – a *comm*ander – this is your manifesto to strategic communications. *The DIY Newsroom* will change your business operations for the better. If you are at the coalface of communications – a *comm*ando – then this is your handbook to instituting such change.

In the local library, this book might sit in the marketing or digital media section. But I like to think it's a book like no other. Fundamentally, *The DIY Newsroom* is about unlocking your unrealised potential – and putting that on show to the world.

Now, are you ready?

– *Stuart Howie*

PART I

THE DIY NEWSROOM EXPLAINED

CHAPTER 1

WHAT *IS* A DIY NEWSROOM?

"What we've got here is failure to communicate."

CAPTAIN, *COOL HAND LUKE,* 1967

The difficulties of finding coherence amid the chaos

Media fragmentation has democratised communications and the potential for all of us to connect on a global basis. This provides wonderful opportunities for businesses and audiences, but has also made for a messy, confusing and overwhelming communications landscape. As consumers of information, it can be like drinking from a fire hose. For organisations trying to stand out from the crowd, the benefit of all the choice and freedom to communicate can be outweighed by the sheer noise created.

Corporates, start-ups, individuals – let's call it *society* – are becoming more frustrated by the day.

The most common communication problems

In business, lack of communications clarity is a killer to motivation, to direction and to success, however that is gauged. Research I've conducted over the past few years reveals three common themes when it comes to trying to get communications cut through. Business leaders tell me:

- **They are overwhelmed.** That is not surprising. The amount of information coming at us has trebled in as many years, according to the International News Media Association.

- **They are not getting a return on their communication efforts.** There is often lots of activity but not a commensurate result, and as a result the great work of the organisation, its teams and individuals goes unrecognised.

- **They understand the need to change at a rational level, but they do not know how to go about it** and there are underlying fears.

With such a changeable environment and swirling emotions, it's unsurprising many businesses make costly mistakes. Inaction is one of them. Leaders get stunned in the headlights and are unable to lock down and pursue a strategy. Or they keep doing what they did in the past, or they just travel with the herd.

Other companies *do* take action, but without a deliberate system or strategy, they go for the scattergun approach, wasting time, energy and money. Or they equate communications success with volume and so produce rubbish content.

Occasionally, a company strikes it lucky by being in the right place at the right time, even if their comms are all over the place.

The solution

The individuals and businesses that typically succeed are those that have a strong brand, produce engaging content, and can convey that on a regular and sustainable basis. They do this by taking a considered approach.

Today, though, breaking through the cacophony of communications means disrupting the norm. This requires a new communications system, a new way that marries the timeless principles of good communications with the advantages presented by technology.

A DIY Newsroom does that by putting communications at the beating heart of what you do. It puts you back in control of your message by providing a method to the madness.

So, when it comes to communications, are you *heard* or *herd*?

What can I learn from a newsroom?

The principles and practices of a newsroom constitute the ultimate guide for communicating effectively.

Why? Because newsrooms are at the top of the content food chain.

Long before content marketing was a concept, newsrooms were feeding news and information to hungry audiences. Quite simply, content is their reason for being. This is what a newsroom does.

Newsrooms have been pressure tested over generations in all sorts of media environments. The best newsrooms are early adopters of technology, which, of course, keeps them ahead of the game. Modern newsrooms have learned valuable lessons from the rise and rise of the internet and now social media.

For any organisation with communications and marketing resources, newsrooms also represent a way of working and a blueprint for mobilising resources.

The DIY Newsroom is not journalism, content marketing, brand marketing, public relations or corporate communications, but it does have elements of each.

Unlike journalism, the DIY Newsroom is out to serve *your* interests. But the content that's produced is more than self-promoting puff and PR. What journalists do better than anyone, and what we learn from them, is the primacy of storytelling. In the DIY Newsroom, you too can create compelling and useful content that gives your organisation greater influence and authority.

A DIY Newsroom can undertake many of the internal and external communications found in a corporate comms environment. And it may resemble content marketing. But content marketing typically lacks integration, focusing instead on isolated campaigns, platforms and digital tools. As well, content marketing is unhealthily obsessed with social media – in fact, the industry is based on it.

There are lots of pretenders and media wannabes out there. And, sure, lots of valuable advice comes from specialists in digital and social media. But rarely is this presented in a systematic or inte-grated fashion – one that is easy to follow. I'm going to pull back the curtain to reveal how you can apply the principles of a newsroom in your world to make your business communications much more effective. I'm going to teach you how to create a DIY Newsroom.

Creating a DIY Newsroom

What do you think of when you hear the words "DIY Newsroom"? You might picture a busy open-plan office with banks of TV screens and a central news desk where animated discussion takes place. And perhaps you think all you need from me is a quick how-to and an Allen key.

Certainly, there are physical attributes of a newsroom that may be worth you and your organisation recreating. However, the DIY Newsroom is more than a physical environment. Rather, it is a way of working and thinking: it's a new approach to communications.

As the name implies, a DIY Newsroom is founded on the practices of news outlets. To relate these practices to a non-media environment, I developed the SMART Way™, which distils what newsrooms do best and lays it out for others to follow. SMART stands for **S**trategy, **M**edia, **A**uthenticity, **R**esults and **T**eam – the five steps to simple, strategic, successful and sustainable communications.

I'll introduce the steps now, and we'll go into them in detail through-out the book:

1. **S**TRATEGY constitutes the blueprint for building the DIY Newsroom.

2. **M**EDIA determines the weapons of mass communication you will deploy in the battle for hearts and minds.

3. **A**UTHENTICITY is the secret sauce for creating content that makes a heartfelt connection with customers and prospects.

4. **R**ESULTS are how you gauge your success.

5. **T**EAM inspires you to mobilise the X-factor, the people who will run your DIY Newsroom.

The sum of these parts – the integration and synchronicity brought by being SMART – is what distinguishes the DIY Newsroom from orthodox communications.

You will be heard

Clarity and results come as the SMART Way is put in place. The first thing you will notice with a DIY Newsroom is that you will become more discerning about the content you produce because you will be crystal clear about the purpose of what you are doing, who you are trying to reach and the best channels for that.

The mechanics of communicating are important. But putting com-munications central in your operations and adopting the SMART Way will fuel your long-term success. The ultimate prize is you will be heard. You will get recognition for your hard work. And you will shine in your sector.

AN EXAMPLE OF A DIY NEWSROOM: BEACONHILLS, A LEADING LIGHT

Beaconhills College in Melbourne's exploding south-eastern suburbs was a "living lab" for the DIY Newsroom.

The college was the perfect client, not the least because its leaders embraced the SMART Way and were studious in applying it – and with stunning results.

The college has some 3000 students, from pre-school to leaving, based at two campuses, and 500 staff. An independent, open-entry school, Beaconhills had grown from humble beginnings in 1982 to developing a reputation for delivering educational excellence at exceptional value.

The college could have been forgiven for riding on its past success. But with increased scale comes new challenges. Student enrolments began to plateau, and the headmaster and marketing director could see the need to rethink their external communications. It was now less clear how to get cut through. And social media and the mobile experience had changed the way school communities were interacting. In short, old-school comms was not working.

My consultancy, Flame Tree Media, began working with Beaconhills to lay a new path.

To its advantage, the college already had a marketing and admissions team of half-a-dozen staff across functions. We met, unpacked all the issues and reviewed existing strengths. Working with the communications coordinator and accomplished former journalist Leigh Parry, we conducted a 101-point health check. Then we went through the rest of the SMART steps in a logical, no-nonsense manner. It was very much as outlined in this book, including conducting an audience identification, auditing content and getting across all social media accounts.

Critically, we re-evaluated the network of channels. We decided to ramp up the use of Facebook, introduced a tighter publishing regime, including the use of Instagram, and identified the alumni community – some thousands of former students – as a golden opportunity to leverage ready-made ambassadors around the world. The strategy, endorsed by the headmaster and board, put video central, but also recognised how traditional comms, like the college's high-quality gloss publications, were still valued by the school community.

The comms team became more discerning and skilled about the content it created and shared. This extended well beyond school notices. The team showed a real "nose for news" in what would interest its audiences, and became even more adept at producing great storytelling across media.

The team required some reorganising, and new tools were introduced so the approach was within its capacity to sustain.

In the background was the awareness that education is a minefield of reputational threats. We have seen even the most elite schools wracked by internal division. Then there are the headline-catching scandals of students or teachers behaving badly, and this being shared via social media. Or worse.

Beaconhills's new way got a workout when it suffered every school's worst nightmare, when police arrived without notice and arrested a teacher. Without getting into the gory details, the recast comms team and its restructured network of media channels meant it was able to inform the school community quickly about the circumstances. Rather than pulling down the shutters – the ostrich approach often taken in these situations – the college front-footed the situation with confidence, all under the pressure of metropolitan media attention and requests. Essentially, the college had a playbook.

Beaconhills's communications transformation is testimony to the variety of benefits that come from taking a strategic approach.

In a little more than 18 months, Facebook engagement and following measurably soared, alumni membership more than doubled, and the college created communities of interest because of its extended use of video and social.

Most significantly, the comms approach well-served the objective of increasing inquiries and enrolments. Strategic marketing drove unprecedented interest in the college's open day, local enrolments spiked again, and staff found themselves with the nice problem of how to deal with mounting interest from international families.

A beaut acknowledgement was when Beaconhills was named a finalist for the SMART Newsroom in the online communications category at the industry's peak EducatePlus awards.

And this is what happens when you take control of your messaging. This is what happens when you get SMART.

CHAPTER 2

WHO SHOULD CREATE A DIY NEWSROOM?

"Change is the law of life. And those who look only to the past or present are certain to miss the future."

US PRESIDENT JOHN F. KENNEDY, 1961

Who this book helps – and how

The CEO of a mid-sized corporation laments that they can't control the public narrative about their business. The leader of a struggling not-for-profit complains they are not getting communications cut-through, but they do not have an email database of their audience and miss a prime opportunity to engage. A director in the education sector wants to exercise greater influence on government policy, but has not developed a social media community and goes unheard. A local government boss wonders why constituents have such animosity towards their organisation, but the council has provided few touchpoints for positive interaction. An umbrella association is lost in the crowd – its content is bland, boring and banal.

In each case, these organisations are doing exceptional things in their field. But they are failing in the public eye or – just as bad – they are invisible. The DIY Newsroom shows organisations how to put the spotlight on their great work, so that these problems are avoided.

For *commanders* …

For the corporate leader – for the *comm*ander – this book is a manifesto. It outlines the principles of the DIY Newsroom and inspires them to create change.

As a leader, you may be a C-suite executive in a large organisation. Or you may be an entrepreneur seeking to kickstart a new business. Either way, this book is a battle plan for winning in the Attention Economy. I tell you how to set up and launch a DIY Newsroom.

For *commandos* …

For the communications practitioner – for the *comm*ando – this book is a guide. It explains the practices of the DIY Newsroom. It tells you how to establish and sustain such an operation.

Marketing and communications is a booming business. It is marked by intense competition and is a constantly moving environment. If you are part of such a team, you want a method that sets you apart from the rest. You may have mastered social media and a mind-blowing array of digital tools, but sometimes your journey feels more like a treadmill than one taking you anywhere meaningful.

This book addresses the central question: how can my communication operations be improved in a simple, strategic and sustainable way to provide my organisation (and me) with greater exposure and immediate results?

Whether you are a *comm*ander or *comm*ando, this is your playbook for SMART communications. It will help you to shine.

What businesses and sectors does a DIY Newsroom suit?

Many businesses in many sectors can benefit from taking a DIY Newsroom approach, customising it for their circumstances and within their capacity. A DIY Newsroom is perfect for organisations with existing marketing and communication resources. Typically, this is medium to large enterprises, but the principles outlined here are timeless standards that can be applied for impact by any sized business or organisation, and even to raise an individual's profile.

Every sector has its communication challenges. But the DIY Newsroom particularly suits organisations that have a sense of purpose about what they do. They might not be changing the entire world, but they do want to make a difference on their patch.

The DIY Newsroom helps organisations and individuals become a voice of authority and thereby an influencer. Big organisations have the money to hire the top advertising agencies and a range of communication experts. But if you analysed this, much of what they do could be done using the organisation's own resources, and with greater impact. I'm not just talking about corporates either. I see plenty of taxpayers' money wasted by government departments. And – sadly – many not-for-profits, who can least afford it, follow the same path of wasting resources.

In the course of researching this book, I found how big institutions were getting SMART and dropping old-school public relations and advertising. Instead, they were seeking to make a heartfelt connection with their audiences and they were doing that by adopting a new approach. New tools and technology have given them this ability to create, distribute and control their message. I saw this at the Australian Football League, at ANZ Bank, and with Australia's largest private health insurer, Bupa. I also see the frustrations of my clients who want more strategically positioned communications.

And media fragmentation means many organisations can no longer rely on what they used to do for promotion.

In this sense, local government is a prime candidate for a DIY Newsroom. Many local newspapers have been shut down or had their resources slashed. The upside is that councils have the opportunity to position themselves as the new community voice – not as a destination for independent local journalism but as the go-to place for a host of local information.

Schools, colleges, universities and trade schools also have the scale and expertise to form a DIY Newsroom. This can position them as thought leaders in the education space, or even just as a distributor of "how to" information. After all, isn't that what schools do? Teach us? Universities have marketing and communications staff scattered across faculties and campuses. Only part of that resource needs to be integrated to form an effective newsroom-style operation.

Sports clubs, from local athletics clubs to international brands such as Manchester United, are recognising the benefits of taking control of their intellectual property. The former are doing it because they are frustrated at trying to get their message out through traditional means. The elite clubs and organisations, such as the AFL, are wanting to optimise their high-profile brands.

What this book is *not*

This book is *not* a guide to social media. I heavily reference social media, but like all technology, it is an enabler and has no purpose in itself. I want this to be a timeless work, and everyone's circumstances will differ.

This book is *not* a content marketing guide. I explain content processes and how to make a campaign sing. I acknowledge the importance of seeking specialist advice where needed. This might be for SEO (search engine optimisation), EDM (email direct marketing) or a CMS (content management system). This book will help you decide if you need further expertise, or any at all, but this is not a technical guide.

This book is *not* an academic work on communications. If it were to become a widely quoted work on communications, that would exceed my expectations. The ultimate flattery, though, would be if you applied what is here and you struck a blow.

This book is *not* about crisis communications. That said, if you have a DIY Newsroom in place you will be well inoculated and prepared for those situations.

Finally, and most importantly, this book is *not* for those unwilling to change. In my experience, many people *say* they are up for change but they rarely appreciate what is involved. In hindsight, leaders often acknowledge that when it comes to change they should have and could have been bolder and quicker. Never underestimate what you and your people can achieve. The DIY Newsroom operates in the spirit of living with no such regrets and unashamedly sets the bar high.

Whether you are a *comm*ander or a *comm*ando, this is your playbook. But I also wrote this book for deeply personal reasons, which you will find out about in the next chapter.

CHAPTER 3

WHY I WROTE THIS BOOK

"Just do it."

NIKE TRADEMARK

Like a rolling stone

I love working with teams and people, and I have always believed in the power of communications and storytelling to make a difference in the world.

It is in my blood.

My father, Bill Howie, was a radio announcer with Melbourne's first radio rock station, 3AK, and this took me into the beating heart of media as it was then. There is a terrific photo of Dad with the Rolling Stones aboard a small boat on Port Phillip Bay in 1966 during a live outside broadcast. I was only a baby at the time, but during the '70s and '80s I got to watch Dad at work in the studio – and I was mesmerised by the magic of the microphone and the ability for it to reach so many people.

At home, I was surrounded by books, records and newspapers. This connected me to the world, and I determined at the age of seven that I wanted to be a reporter. I began to produce my own newspapers and sent them to relatives in England. I was already a media junkie, and I was going global.

Bush papers and beyond

On leaving high school, I started work as a cadet journalist at a small country newspaper. The newsroom comprised me and the chain-smoking editor. I covered three local councils, police, courts and general rounds. I collated sports results over the weekend. I juggled a notebook with the office camera. Between puffs on his cigarette, "Brocky", the editor, explained F-stops and how the flash worked to a bewildered, peroxide-haired 18-year-old.

If I got anything wrong in an edition I would soon know about it. I saw most of our contacts down the street – in the bakery, at the supermarket and at the fish 'n' chip shop. Shire councillors would give Brocky an ear-bashing at the pub when I wrote a negative story.

I loved it.

I was making an impression on the world, even if my part of the world was a sparsely populated country backblock.

This launched me into the wild and wondrous world of journalism. I went on to edit my local paper, and then bigger papers – regional dailies – and for a while I was the acting editor of *The Canberra Times*.

I explored the wider world through two fellowships. The first one, in 1996, took me through the US, where the internet was starting to have an impact on media. A few years later, I was in newspaper heaven as I toured and worked on British newspapers as a fellow with the Commonwealth Press Union.

I was ambitious, but mainly for doing the best that I could and making a contribution within the communities I worked.

After 30 years of reporting and editing, mostly for newspapers, it was time for a change of direction – from a relentless schedule of deadlines to having a wider strategic influence. As Editorial Director of Fairfax Media's mammoth regional network, I became a student of strategy. This was an opportunity to make a difference in a new way, especially as the panic had set in around the future of newspapers.

We had 180 regional and rural newspapers, and I oversaw some 800 journalists. The challenge was to establish a new business model that relied less on print. This excited me because I had the chance to reinvent our newspapers (they were still profitable) and design a digital-first strategy, embodied in a project I called NewsNow. After much internal resistance, the managing director supported the plan, honed by my small team – and we were off. This gave me the opportunity to visit newsrooms across Australia and to evangelise a new way. I was a pig in mud.

But, having done the spade work and given the business a new editorial direction, it was the perfect time to leave the company. To move to "civilian life".

Going my own way

After 17 years, I left Fairfax on a Friday. That same day, my company Flame Tree Media was incorporated, and on the Monday I flew to New Zealand to listen to the problems of my first client.

It was time to help others transform their businesses.

Since then I have worked with big corporates, national organisations, schools, sporting associations, churches and not-for-profits. I have spoken at universities and conferences, prepared communications for international events, designed and run workshops, developed content and transformation strategies, worked on business cases, run large cross-functional projects, judged awards in Australia and overseas, spoken on webinars, and developed my own media eco-system of videos, blogs, brochures – and now this book.

Whether I'm working in a newsroom to help management transform operations or in a corporate environment coaching a team, the work I do is about helping people tell their stories. To find their voice.

One of my maxims is "don't hide your light under a bushel [bowl]". It comes from the Sermon on the Mount, and it means that when you have something great that others should know about, make sure everyone can see it.

In supporting organisations in this way, I see myself as a true brand ambassador for their businesses – and indeed for them personally. I love nothing than to lift that bowl and let them shine.

PART II

WHAT YOU NEED TO KNOW ABOUT THE INFORMATION ECONOMY

CHAPTER 4

UNDERSTANDING COMMUNICATION AND THE MEDIA

"History will be kind to me for I intend to write it."

WINSTON CHURCHILL

What *is* effective communication?

Aristotle's framework of ethos, pathos and logos is still regarded as the central structure for effective public speaking, which in Ancient Greece was the primary public relations channel.

Aristotle (384–322 BC) was the father of science. While some of his thinking has been unpicked thousands of years later, Aristotle's contribution across disciplines – including logic, maths, biology, dance and theatre – is unsurpassed in history. As a student of Plato and teacher of Alexander the Great, Aristotle was an A-list celebrity of his time.

In *The Art of Rhetoric,* Aristotle identified the three essentials to powerful communications:

1. *Ethos:* establishing credibility or authority on a matter.

2. *Pathos:* making an emotional connection with the audience.

3. *Logos:* appealing to people's sense of reasoning.

Aristotle's model recognised the need for arresting content, and to craft and deliver that information in a way that resonated with the audience emotionally and intellectually.

Subsequent communication models were more expansive, taking into account two-way communication and the potential for numerous channels. In the 1940s, American sociologist Harold Lasswell deconstructed communication activities into a simple formula:

- who … (the communicator)
- says what … (the message)
- in which channel … (the medium)
- to whom … (the receiver)
- with what effect.

The last point about effect is important. As Walt Seifert, a professor emeritus of public relations at Ohio State University, observed about a communication:

Dissemination does not equal publication, and publication does not equal absorption and action. All who receive it won't publish it, and all who read or hear won't understand or act upon it.

How we process information

New media methods, channels and technology let us tickle more senses with our communications.

Researchers have tried to quantify what amount of information we retain from individual senses. One stream of thought is that our brains process visual information ahead of that from any of our other senses, while American researcher and educator Edgar Dale developed the "cone of experience" in the 1940s whereby he reasoned we learn from doing. Others have attributed percentages to Dale's work, along the lines that we remember:

- 90 per cent of what we do
- 70 per cent of what we say and write
- 50 per cent of what we see and hear
- 30 per cent of what we see
- 20 per cent of what we hear
- only 10 per cent of we read.

We continue to learn more about the workings of the brain. However, it is accepted we absorb information best when we are immersed in an experience. As the Chinese proverb goes:

I hear and I forget.
I read and I remember.
I do and I understand.

What does this mean for us? It indicates strongly that experiential technologies such as augmented and virtual reality will be part of the *comm*ando's arsenal of the future. It supports too the increasing role video will have.

This is not to denigrate the written word (hey, I'm writing a book). Later, I talk about the power of print. But we have surely established we can no longer just hit the receiver in a communication with a wall of words. And for every message we have to share with an audience, there is an optimum way to do that.

This is obvious to comms professionals, but to make that second nature for others requires considered thought – and a plan.

Mastering your message

US President John Fitzgerald Kennedy was an exceptional orator, and shaped public opinion like few others have in modern times. He was intelligent and charismatic. But his biggest asset was technology: television.

His press secretary Pierre Salinger, interviewed for the John F. Kennedy Library, outlined the tactic to go direct with live press conferences:

> *When President Kennedy started televised press conferences there were only three or four newspapers in the entire United States that carried a full transcript of a presidential press conference. Therefore, what people read was a distillation ... We thought that they should have the opportunity to see it in full.*

The Kennedy Administration reached into every home with a compelling narrative about a reimagined America.

Old-school marketing and communications

If you want to be media-ocre, do what everyone has been doing for a few decades in public relations. You still see it as PR agencies charge like a wounded bull, working furiously to get mentions for clients in print or appearances on radio and TV.

I would be the last person to deny the value of getting a run in traditional media because of the authority and exposure it brings your brand. However, the formula for success is more involved today. If your communication centres on the following, then it is time to change:

- sending media releases on product releases or service launches to mainstream media in the hope they are covered
- sending promotional packs and gifts to journalists hoping they write about your products
- wining and dining
- buying newspaper "advertorial space".

Let's have a look at where the action is today.

News, advertising and the murky bit in between

Like church and state, there has always been a clear demarcation between the editorial and advertising departments of news outlets. In many cases, advertising staff were not even permitted in newsrooms lest they try to (unsuccessfully) seek favourable coverage for their clients.

Advertising was the blatant sell of a product or service. This space or air time needed to be bought. News was the credible stuff, produced by journalists who were ferociously independent and could not be swayed by fear nor favour. There were well-accepted journalistic standards – as there are today, despite what the public sometimes thinks of reporters.

I still recall fondly the crusading motto of my first paper, *The Seymour Telegraph*: "Truth Without Fear". Along the same lines, the great British media baron Lord Northcliffe (Alfred Harmsworth) was attributed as saying: "News is what somebody somewhere wants to suppress, all the rest is advertising".

Because of the rigour and standards of journalism, it has greater credibility than advertising. For that reason, PR firms and advertisers have always sought to get or plant positive mentions in the media – which is more valuable than any full-page ad or radio commercial.

As a compromise, media outlets have provided businesses with something like a news experience via "advertorials" – an editorial that is essentially advertising. For instance, an advertiser might pay for a full page in a newspaper, with a half-page ad and then content shaped as editorial. This content might be supplied direct by the business, by an agency, or written by the newspaper's advertorial or "creative services" team. If you were a journalist and you were made to work in this team, it was no less than being transferred to the Siberian desert. There was no lower rung in journalism.

Radio and TV have offered similar advertorial environments. While such content must meet industry regulation, it can be hard to distinguish it from "real news". In this vein, we have also seen the growth of online sponsored and branded content.

The great communications con

Why is this important to understand? Because this grey zone, the open field between straight news and advertising, is at the epicentre of the war for attention today. It's busy with seasoned professionals and awful amateurs blazing away with bazookas and not having a clue about their target. This zone represents a multi-gazillion dollar marketplace – and it has seen the rise and rise of one of the greatest cons perpetrated on the corporate world: content marketing.

The rise and rise of content marketing has occurred in parallel with the empowering nature of social media. Content marketing is one of the world's fastest growing industries, and is forecast to be worth US$300 billion by 2019.

The industry is founded on the same problems the DIY Newsroom seeks to address. Content marketing is about creating stories about your business and sharing them across platforms to support your reach and influence.

Some content marketers do a tremendous job of providing a communications framework and instructing businesses how to do it themselves. Joe Pulizzi, the founder and CEO of the Content Marketing Institute in the US, is one of the pioneers of the content marketing industry and personifies the positives.

But many content companies do not seem to have any wider vision – rather, they opportunistically latch onto an aspect of communications and make a business of that. This includes:

- video creation and production
- content (words) creation and production
- social media (posting, listening, moderation and management)
- website design and management
- search engine optimisation (SEO)
- analytics and reporting
- campaigns
- brand marketing and graphic design.

This is not to say do not go and buy expertise – say, for that piece of video for your brand marketing, to push a particular campaign, to provide you with a Google Adwords strategy, or to give you some extra grunt to rewrite web content to meet a deadline. But, as the Romans said, *caveat emptor* – beware the buyer.

The net impact of misfiring content marketing can be:

- needlessly spending money for likes or shares that could go towards more meaningful and lasting communications
- wasting focus, time and energy on non-strategic initiatives
- a fragmented approach.

The best content marketing is about creating a holistic environment for products or services. That does not sound very viral, but it is SMART.

I regularly wonder why companies choose to outsource the biggest thing they have going for them for others to interpret: their reason for being. Usually, they have the expertise themselves to communicate what they are all about.

Better communications

The good news is that a DIY Newsroom does most of what content marketing does but puts it in context. The DIY Newsroom is about the new space. It means you are not fighting it out in that murky middle ground. Rather, you are creating your story and telling it on your terms.

The new way to engage your tribes, as marketer Seth Godin would describe audiences, is by:

- creating a content community and being recognised as a thought leader
- using a variety of media and distribution methods to relay precise messaging
- external media seeking you out because they have read your blogs, seen your videos, engaged with your social posts and know you are the go-to expert in your niche.

This makes for a connection with audiences as timeless as Aristotle's teachings. And it recognises the tumultuous times of today.

CHAPTER 5

HOW MEDIA GOT MASHED AND REHASHED

"In the future, everyone will be world famous for 15 minutes."

ANDY WARHOL

The digital big bang

As much as digital disruption is seen as a phenomenon of the past decade, it had its origins in the 1990s.

Typically, the development and mainstreaming of technology follows consumer demand. To that end, we can pinpoint 1993 – the year Bill Clinton was sworn in as US President and Intel shipped the first Pentium chips – as one of those milestones. It was then that the internet transitioned from a defence and government network to one accessible to the general public – as we know it, the world wide web.

As the '90s progressed, the internet's tentacles began reaching into our lives. Amazon was established in 1994, Google in 1998, and six years later (yes, well after MySpace) Facebook began. Steve Jobs founded Apple during the 1970s, but it was not until the 1990s that the company's product lines took shape, marked by Jobs's return to the company in 1997.

Other companies have helped shape our information economy, but the four tech titans – Amazon, Google, Facebook and Apple – have blown up life as we know it. They are mainly, though not entirely, responsible for the massive fragmentation of media and information services.

The impact? Consider:

- In 2017, Facebook and Google were responsible for nearly 80 per cent of news publishers' traffic.
- Together, they claimed (depending on the source) between 60 and 90 per cent of every new online ad dollar in America.
- Facebook, at last count, is the world's biggest content platform, with more than 2.1 billion monthly users, giving it the world's largest pool of personal data (ouch).
- Google dominates as much as 85 per cent of online/search/ad revenue globally.

- Amazon controls 40 per cent of America's online commerce, and it is only just starting in countries like Australia.

This has occurred in the lifetime of our kids.

As a society, we have allowed these tech titans to control how we communicate, shop, do business, think, and live our lives. Why? Because, fundamentally, we love the experiences they provide. It's an avalanche of information we have brought down on ourselves.

Traditional media's big crunch

Early on, you could see that the internet would radically disrupt media, although we had no inkling of the breadth and depth.

I travelled to the US on a newspaper fellowship in 1996, Palm Pilot firmly in hand, as media began to grapple with that first wave of change. It was not the end of newspapers, as some thought it to be. But, to channel Churchill, it was the beginning of the end of those halcyon days and the start of something, well, different.

As a young editor of suburban newspapers in Melbourne, I could see how American executives were already trying to re-focus their business models. In my report "Grassroots News" for the Australian Suburban Newspaper Association I stated:

> *The future of news companies lies in their ability to adapt. The internet, depending who you speak to, is going to kill newspapers, put multitudes of journalists out of jobs, or it's the brave new world of untapped and unlimited opportunities. It is clear it is going to open up many doors for how companies present that product of local news and advertising and for them to extend their reach. As for the future? It is here. Most American newspapers, even the most conservative, are getting online. The big question is how do you make money from the internet?*

More than 20 years later, the jury is finally in: the local advertising model as we know it is dead. Digital advertising, for the most part, is a mirage – unless you are Facebook and Google. Game over. You do not make money from the internet. Well, not for just being *on* the internet.

Instead, news outlets, for the most part, have had to diversify their businesses to fund their journalism because few have the critical mass to support it, even with paywalls – a notable exception being the *New York Times* with a few million digital subscribers and aiming for 10 million.

Many of the companies I visited 20 years ago have changed hands, merged, closed or been bought out by private equity. Resources were not a problem then, but every surviving media outlet has in recent times had to slash costs and raze unnecessary business activities. The profitability of journalism has increasingly been in the spotlight, although thanks to Donald J. Trump it found a renewed public value.

Harvard Business Review reported that media was the most disrupted of any industry in 2015. As dangerous as it is to state, this disruption appears to have peaked. This only means today's communications chaos has become the norm. Victory will go to those who can best piece together a way, a process, amid the new world disorder.

The Toxic Information Chain

Media fragmentation has caused what I call the Toxic Information Chain (TIC):

- The democratisation of information distribution has made it possible for anyone to reach an audience. You do not need a multi-million-dollar printing press, TV studio or radio station.
- Such information can be amplified like never before. Quite the journey since the days of Aristotle.
- Because it is self-serve, anyone can say anything.

- It goes to follow that such information may be seen and believed – and the system can be gamed and manipulated (the Russians will show you how). Hence, we have seen the controversy around "fake news", both real and perceived.
- This has lowered the standard of information across social media platforms and society in general.
- This has lowered the perceived standard of journalism as it has been lumped in with the social media morass.
- This has almost destroyed the traditional media model and the ability to support real news, further amplifying the work of amateurs, info-crooks and time wasters.

But ... there is an upside

Despite all the mayhem wrought by social media, the gatekeepers to having your message heard no longer exist. There is no sweating on whether a local editor will cover your story or having to fork out big bucks to advertise in a glossy magazine. Smart businesses have the ability to control their own message and, to a good extent, their business destiny. Media fragmentation has made it easier to distribute information more cheaply, quickly and effectively.

CHAPTER 6

THE SEVEN TITANIC MISTAKES OF COMMUNICATIONS

"There is no danger that Titanic *will sink.
The boat is unsinkable ..."*

PHILLIP FRANKLIN, WHITE STAR LINE
VICE PRESIDENT, 1912

More than 100 years on, the sinking of the *Titanic* remains that quintessentially gripping disaster story. The so-called "unsinkable" ship struck an iceberg near midnight on 14 April, 1912, broke in two and sunk with the loss of 1517 lives.

It was man-versus-nature, but with the benefit of hindsight the tragedy could have been avoided. Critically, the ocean liner's crew should have heeded warnings from other vessels of the icebergs that lay ahead. As history records, the *Titanic* kept on at full pace, eager to make New York on time. By the time lookout Frederick Fleet spotted the iceberg it was too late; the ship had barely 40 seconds to take evasive action.

Today, ships have the benefit of a variety of smarts – satellite technology, digital navigation and radar – which ensures the safety of those at sea.

We too need to use our smarts when it comes to targeting what we do in communications.

Don't scuttle your communications before you leave dock

In my experience, there are Seven Titanic Mistakes that will scuttle your communication operations before you even leave dock. They are remarkably common, but the good news is they can be avoided. I'll show you how to do so in this book. You also need to make sure you avoid these issues while you are building your DIY Newsroom.

So, here's the Seven Titanic Mistakes of Communications:

1. **Spending money unnecessarily:** The reality is that many marketing budgets are poorly managed or directed. This raises the ire of CEOs, CMOs and CFOs, who complain about the resources spent on campaigns that do not provide a tangible benefit to the business. Or money is spent on campaigns that

create a fleeting buzz, but like any sugar-hit the result dissipates quickly.

2. **Producing rubbish content:** Every day, on every platform, on every feed, I see content that is bland, boring and banal. Creating a community requires quality content. Much of what you see on social media is repetitive. What resonates is content that provides the audience with insights or solutions to their problems, supported by real results and compelling personal stories or case studies. And, gee, loosen the tie and show some personality rather than blending in with the rest of the very crowded web scene. Show flair. Be original. Craft amazingly independently minded campaigns.

3. **Ignoring the X-factor:** Typically, only about 10 per cent of an iceberg is visible. In the *Titanic*'s case, that was almost 70 million tonnes of rock-hard Greenland ice. We can fail to see that our biggest asset is sitting right next to us – the people who run our comms teams who have immense experience. We just have to inspire them and turn on the tap for creative output. Is your team as inspired or as well-functioning as it should be? Is it structured to meet the needs of your audiences? Do you provide them with the training, coaching, equipment and encouragement needed to excel at what they do?

4. **Not acting strategically:** Developing strategy takes time, expertise and resources, which is counterintuitive for these fast-paced times where agility and snap decisions are the go. But, as I outline in my SMART Way, disorganisation is death.

5. **Going scattergun:** The common scattergun approach is the result of not being strategic. This means jumping at every shiny new toy. Most of the time you will miss the mark – and it is exhausting. Going scattergun also shows up your naivety and puts you on a direct path to a Titanic disaster, maybe to your own career as those around you wonder what the heck your plan is.

6. **Not valuing communications:** Not everyone gets the need to communicate. There are still some sectors and some bosses for whom communication ranks low. This could be because they come from the "no news is good news" school of communications. Or they believe their sector does not have communications sex appeal. Or they have never thought to build their organisation around a community of content. In such circumstances, comms teams need to show the powers-that-be the strong WIIFM (what's-in-it-for-me) factor. Failing that, ring-a-ding-ding – iceberg ahead.

7. **Not controlling your own distribution:** Behind not acting strategically, I think this is the greatest and most deadly mistake comms teams can make – surrendering all to social. Yes, social media can and does bring great reach for organisations. But that should not be the sum total of your communications strategy, not the least because ever-changing algorithms can in a heartbeat relegate you and your connections from hero to zero. Facebook, LinkedIn, Twitter and other platforms espouse lofty ideals about making the world a better place by connecting us all, but they are there to turn a profit. Having built their own audiences, they are aggressively moving to an advertising model. The free ride is over and you now have to pay for reach. Understand too, the web is only going to get busier. The wisest strategy is to build a loyal following across your own platforms, such as on your website, blog, or via email marketing, and use social media in a discerning way to support those endeavours.

You cannot expect smooth sailing as communication techniques evolve exponentially. But avoiding these seven classic mistakes will steer you away from trouble and put you ahead of the pack.

CHAPTER 7

THE SIRENS OF SOCIAL MEDIA

"Now stop your ship and listen to our voices.
All those who pass this way hear honeyed song,
poured from our mouths"

HOMER, *THE ODYSSEY*

Social media's impact on our lives

Teenage daughter. Smartphone. Toilet. Not a good combination. We had told her relentlessly not to take the phone into the toilet. But kids … sheesh.

The phone had bobbed around in the toilet for a good while until a girlfriend at the party noticed something that did not flush. Apparently, said daughter had the phone in her back pocket when she went to the bathroom. Amazingly, the phone recovered after being packed in rice for a day. And it was not too long until my daughter was back to her old ways, taking the phone with her *everywhere*. Grrr.

The statistics show her behaviour is common. More of us are using our phones more often, mostly for social media, and we are now doing so where it once was taboo: at the cinema, in school, in restaurants. According to the Sensis Social Media Report, 14 per cent of

Australians admitted to using their phone while in the toilet, with men worse offenders than women.

Mobile use and social media go hand in hand. More than 80 per cent of us use smartphones as the device of choice to access social media. *The Economist* reported that users in affluent countries touched their smartphones 2600 times a day.

More of us are using social media

Social media use, however, is yet to reach saturation point. At last count, 79 per cent of the Australian population used social media – up 10 points on the previous year. The World Economic Forum's Global Agenda Council on Social Media estimates about 2.5 billion people use social networks, 2.5 times the number at the start of the decade.

Social media was formerly the domain of the young – millennials. Now it's finding broader appeal across the ages, and has roped in Gen Xers and baby boomers. In less than 10 years, the percentage of online adults using social media has increased from 46 per cent to 70 per cent, according to the Pew Research Center. I'm sure you have friends and family who asserted "I don't do social media" but they have succumbed because of FOMO (fear of missing out).

We are spending longer on social media

German-based online researcher and marketer Statista reports the amount of time on social networking increased from 90 minutes per day in 2012 to 135 minutes in 2017.

Really? More than two hours of every day?

Well, a GroupM study in 2017 found users in Britain and Hong Kong spent four to five hours per day on social media. Another researcher, Mediakix, extrapolated that at those rates the average person will spend more than five years of their life on social media – more time than they spend eating, drinking, grooming and (real) socialising.

As well, increasingly we use social media for purposes other than just socialising, checking our news feeds or sharing information. It has also become a way we access and use other services – as a messenger service, for customer service and to make transactions.

It's changing our brains

Something has to give. And it has – scientists have found social media is rewiring our brains.

To accommodate our smartphone and social media addiction, we are trying to make the days run longer by sleeping less. Medical research shows that young people need about nine hours of sleep a night. However, a US study found more than 40 per cent of teens are sleeping less than seven hours because they are spending sneaky time with their smartphone. Adults are as guilty, going to bed with the phone and waking up with it.

Most disturbingly, this constant interaction with social media is changing the plasticity of our brains – namely the nucleus accumbens, which are activated by that sort of stuff. Other research shows the increase in technology use is decreasing students' ability to read and speak to others clearly. And that 18-year-olds now have the social maturity of much younger teens because they have been so locked onto their mobile phones and not engaged in human interaction. New parents are advised that children should have no screen time until at least the age of three.

If you sense that social media has become a drug of dependence, then you are on the right track. We experience dopamine highs from likes and shares, similar to how drug addicts experience a rush. In Australia, young people are banned from entering rooms where there are poker machines, but every day kids are playing their own little slot machines as they "pull to refresh". They – we – are as hooked as any junkie and, without being melodramatic, we are losing our minds to the allure.

But people do not trust social – and they shouldn't

The weird thing is that, despite spending so much time on social media, we do not trust it. Even the highest users of social media recognise that a lot of what they see is tosh – and they are more likely to trust information on social platforms that comes via traditional media sources. As much as we have turned our back on traditional media, we still believe it is far more credible. A 2017 US study found only 37 per cent of Americans trusted what they saw on social media – half the percentage of people who trusted print media.

We should not trust social media. Unlike mainstream media, social media lacks validation and verification – it is one big steaming stew where the finest morsels are hard to distinguish from the cheapest cuts.

Facebook asserts its mission is to "give people the power to build community and bring the world closer together". Yet Facebook has been mired in scandals. It has passed on our information and data to dodgy third parties, as occurred when the consultancy Cambridge Analytica used personal data for political targeting during the 2016 US presidential election and for the Brexit campaign.

Most famously, the Russians infiltrated the US elections via Facebook. Reported *The Economist*: "Facebook has estimated that Russian content on its network, including posts and paid ads, reached 126 million Americans, around 40 per cent of the nation's population". As well, savvy governments and movements have used social media as part of their playbook for propaganda and espionage. At its worst, Facebook was used to help spark the ethnic cleansing of the Rohingya people in Myanmar.

The social media worm is turning

Thankfully, we have become more questioning about what social media brings to the table and its impact on society. This has led to calls for greater reporting and regulation of social media. Germany, for instance, has introduced huge penalties for those who spread hate speech via social media. Facebook has hired thousands of moderators to raise its credibility and to avert the intervention of governments. Artificial intelligence is also being used to monitor and censor untoward activity.

But the genie is out of the bottle. New media has created the Attention Economy where the consumers' time is the currency. This has been sold and traded to the benefit of Silicon Valley. According to Statista, in every minute on the internet, 15 million text messages are sent, four million YouTube videos are watched, half a million photos are shared on Snapchat, and 103 million spam emails are sent.

Perhaps the worst of it is how social media serves as one big echo chamber, amplifying views and prejudices. Are we seeing the bigger picture anymore, that tapestry we call life?

Your social media odyssey

One of my favourite books is *The Odyssey*, the Greek epic of Odysseus who is seeking to find his way home after the battle of Troy. Along the way he is serenaded by the Sirens. These mythical creatures, depicted as beautiful women, sing out to passing sailors. If they do not avoid the Sirens' spell they are lured into shipwreck and certain death.

Social media is like that. You may not have to tie yourself to a ship mast to avoid the allure, but you do need to draw on powers of resistance and think carefully about where you are heading.

To continue the nautical theme, this relates to one of the Seven Titanic Mistakes of Communications: not controlling your main channels. Many organisations come unstuck, serenaded by the Sirens of social media and losing their way.

Social media in a DIY Newsroom

The dangers associated with totally socially led communications is one reason to be dubious about a lot of content marketing. That said, anyone involved in mass communications cannot ignore the potential reach and influence provided by social media. Like the printing press, telegraph, radio and television, social media has redefined our personal and business communications. We are not going back.

In a DIY Newsroom, social media can help you to:

- galvanise a virtual community around content
- go direct to an audience
- with the right content mix, approach and strategy, build trust and desire
- coordinate the scheduling of your communications across channels
- orchestrate online campaigns
- respond to issues and distribute content at scale and immediately.

But be prepared for the negatives. Social media can also:

- give trolls access to you and your operations
- enable people to flame you publicly
- distract you and your team
- demand you spend money for reach
- force you to invest time into moderating
- create a divide between the famous and non-famous in your sector, not necessarily between those who deserve recognition and those who do not
- require you to constantly update your knowledge, skills and technology
- drive you into crisis.

In developing your social media strategy, put yourself in your prospects' position. What gives them the best impression of your organisation's work? What content would grab their attention, and more importantly help to inform, educate or entertain them? How can you use social media in your sales pipeline? What can you give your audiences of value – for nothing?

In social, less is more – less volume but content that is rich in quality and usefulness.

A Moz/BuzzSumo analysis of more than one million internet articles found most content was ignored because people were inept at creating and/or amplifying their content. Of 100,000 Facebook posts, more than 50 per cent received two or fewer shares, likes or comments. Consider how that human resource could have been ploughed into more meaningful activities. The study also found content that was both shared and liked was typically authoritative, fact-based and opinion forming – the sort of quality content a DIY Newsroom produces.

Seven social media faux pas

Here are seven common mistakes organisations make with their social media:

1. Not getting involved because it is "too hard", "too confronting" or "we don't believe in it".
2. Getting too involved and going scattergun – firing off in all directions.
3. Using the wrong delivery mechanism and/or platform and entirely missing the intended target.
4. Being inconsistent in tone, message and timing.
5. Distributing content that jars with the business ethos.
6. Sabotaging the brand with rubbish content or spamming.
7. Not having a content strategy from the outset.

CHAPTER 8

FIVE FORCES POWERING CONTENT TODAY

*"The ocean is a supreme metaphor for change.
I expect the unexpected but am never fully prepared."*

AUTHOR TIM WINTON

Surfing the waves of change

One of the joys of living in Australia is that we are blessed with an endless array of beaches. This has generated a surf culture that has woven itself into community life. It's not uncommon for tradespeople to down tools at lunch and head to the local break for a quick, invigorating surf.

I am not a surfer, but one thing I have learned from them is how adept they are at reading the forces of nature. One way they do that is by identifying rips or channels that take them out as quick as possible to the action. It beats pounding headlong into the surf.

This is a good metaphor for how we can find our way in the sea of communications today. For me, there are five important forces of change we need to understand. These do not comprise the sum total of what is happening across media and communications, but they do take us out to the action and will divide the winners from the wannabes.

Let's have a look …

The rise of data

One of my favourite scenes from the Netflix political drama *House of Cards* is when Aidan Macallan, the data junkie, strips off and dances as his computers churn through a never-ending stream of numbers that determine the fortunes of those lusting for power. How prophetic given Facebook's Cambridge Analytica scandal was yet to unravel.

You do not have to be campaigning for the White House to see the rising value of data, though. At the most basic level in our businesses, an email database is gold. Companies that smartly leverage analytics, tracking, insights, SEO and similar will be the ones that retain and grow an audience, as opposed to companies that waste time on lost causes. Big companies are at an advantage because of their resources and systems. But partnering with third parties can help smaller operators become savvy, results-focused content curators.

Evolving social media

Social media platforms have progressively put the squeeze on the organic reach of brands and businesses. Facebook's algorithm changes have by and large reflected this. The *Chicago Tribune*, as an example, found that despite posting more than ever they received less engagement. Communication professionals, therefore, need to be totally across the upside and pitfalls of social media and how best to use it.

Accelerating change

I still recall the words of *The Wall Street Journal*'s Chief Innovation Officer Edward Rousseau, who told our study group in New York there was not time for an iota of complacency; the pace of change would only multiply. His mantra was "get going, move fast, break silos". A couple of blocks away at the *New York Times*, CEO Mark Thompson mused to us that he had never seen any business at risk of failing by moving too quickly. Perpetual change sounds like a cliché, similar to "the only constant is change". However, we need to be aware change will step up to a new frenetic level.

The rise and rise of mobile

All communication delivery must now be seen through the small window of a smartphone. By 2020, 80 per cent of the world will be connected by smartphones. Already, every Australian spends an average of 28 hours per month on a smartphone (Nielsen). Manufacturers continue to add improvements, and the next generation of smartphones will see additional functionality around audio and visual recognition – less keying, more talking.

I also note two sub-themes:

- **Mobile journalism:** I talk about this in chapter 19, but get excited. Mojo is taking journalism back to the streets.
- **Video:** The emphasis is on "production-light" video, which means keeping it sharp, simple and engaging.

Take video, take mobile, and you have a killer content combination.

Quality is in

Hallelujah. Quality is back in fashion. In recent years, social media has lowered the bar on our expectations. Because anyone could publish, anyone did. But people are now voting with their devices and seeking out authoritative sources on the topics that interest them – and they want to hear from experts, not pretenders. Data-driven technology will channel this content to them. For communicators, that is a call to arms to stop wasting people's time with the mundane and instead work harder to craft campaigns that show flair and originality.

* * *

As you can see, this list is a mix of technology and consumer trends – intel the modern newsroom can use to maximise its impact.

PART III

INSIDE A NEWSROOM

CHAPTER 9

PULLING BACK THE VEIL

"All The News That's Fit To Print."

NEW YORK TIMES MOTTO

The mystery of the newsroom

It stumped me why more communication teams have not imported the best practices of newsrooms; after all, many comms people are ex-journalists. Then it struck me – newsroom staff have been immensely protective of their patch forever. Just as the Freemasons do not talk openly about their secret ways, so too journalists have been protective about what happens in the newsroom.

This stems a little from arrogance, perhaps, as in "civilians" would not understand, and a sense of specialness journalists have about what happens in a newsroom. Indeed, there is a level of secret squirrel when it comes to how news comes together.

You realise newsrooms are a different place to work when you see the reaction of visitors. Their heads swivel in curiosity. Occasionally, I would have visitors sit in on news meetings – and they would be wide-eyed, mouths agape, as robust discussions took place about the events of the day. I'm sure many of them left wondering what they had witnessed.

Some newsrooms still observe a strict division of "church and state" – editorial on the higher ground (sometimes literally, on a higher floor) and sales in its own area. Commercial staff are not permitted in many instances to liaise with journalists, who must be seen to be immune from influence. Sales staff are banned in some newsrooms, and I have worked in places where even general managers have had to tread carefully for fear of incurring the wrath of the editor.

Out of sight and out of mind

Another reason why there is mystery around newsrooms is that, as much as they have been a central place in our communities, they have had to be roped off from the public for security reasons. I have run newsrooms where front counter staff and I have contended with irate and sometimes violent members of the public. Journalists are regularly subject to verbal and physical attack. The slaying of five people at the *Capital Gazette* in Maryland was a recent extreme and tragic example.

Terrorism has brought this into acute focus, most notoriously with the attack on the Paris news magazine *Charlie Hebdo*. Today, like most modern offices, visitors need to be signed in and escorted into a newsroom. Some offices, like *The New York Times*, will not let you anywhere near the newsroom unless you have direct business with staff.

All this has meant that many organisations that would benefit from learning the ways of a newsroom have never had the opportunity. Newsrooms have been out of sight and out of mind.

My mission is to bring them into focus.

For more than 200 years, newsrooms have delivered news and information to audiences in a variety of ways, stimulating the senses and sparking conversations and social change. Because of the nature of what they do – day in, day out – they have mastered the art of consistency and process.

There are physical and structural aspects that make them unique. They have a buzz that is hard to find elsewhere. Mainly, though, it is intangible attributes that distinguish a newsroom. By mimicking those aspects, communication teams can raise their stocks in the content food chain.

So, let's go inside, into the beating heart of the newsroom.

Taking it to the people

The closer your connection to the community the more it makes sense to embed yourself where it all happens.

TV networks do a good job of this, despite the risks of live broadcasting. Fox News in New York and Seven Network in Sydney, both located in their respective CBDs, are proud to have their studios on display to passers-by. We get to peek at the razzle dazzle – the studio and its celebrities.

In the UK and New Zealand, journalists from small town newspapers are taking to the streets, setting up at cafés, libraries, shopping malls and in council buildings. One of the reasons journalists are going mobile is that some community newspaper offices have been closed because of cost pressures.

What could your communications people do to become more publicly accessible and impactful? How would the public benefit from seeing your operations?

CHAPTER 10

THE NEWSROOM SET UP

"I have no special talents. I am only passionately curious."

ALBERT EINSTEIN

My beating heart

My heart beats faster when I walk into a newsroom. I love them. The good, the bad and the ugly.

Getting up close and personal to media has been a thing for me since I was a kid and I watched my father broadcast from the radio station. I got to play in the record library and wander through the adjacent TV studios. Celebrities, lights, cameras – it was all happening. Mostly, I enjoyed watching the news being read on radio or shot on TV.

I still get a rush when I walk into a newsroom. The big ones are what I imagine the White House situation room to be like, with a sense of urgency, snap decision making and passionate conversation.

One of my career highlights was to visit *The Sun* in London some 20 years ago. *The Sun*, owned by Rupert Murdoch's News International, is known for a lot of things. Many within the industry and in the wider population look down on *The Sun*. For me, it was the best of the UK's "red tops", named as such because of their fire-engine red mastheads. Its news team included beyond-clever headline writers. Each day, staff produced a punchy package that tabloids around the world tried to emulate for style and controversy. The banter in the newsroom was extraordinary. I recall the sign above the door to the newsroom: "You are about to enter Sun country". I hope it is still there.

I have visited dozens of other newsrooms over the years. In the UK, I have visited the BBC, Thomson Reuters, *The Guardian* and *The Observer*. I did a short stint as part of a fellowship at the *Liverpool Echo*. In the US, another fellowship took me into the *San Francisco Chronicle*, *Chicago Tribune*, *The Boston Globe*, *The Indianapolis Star* and small community newspapers across the mid-west and on the east coast. I sat in on news conferences, including at the *Milwaukee Journal Sentinel* on the day President Bill Clinton and German Chancellor Helmut Kohl were in town. In 2017, I spent time again in the US and visited *The New York Times*, Bloomberg and *The Wall Street Journal*. I got to see how newsroom starts-ups tick at places like ProPublica. In my role as editorial director for Australian regional newspapers and later as a consultant, I have gotten to work in and see dozens of other newsrooms across Australia and New Zealand.

I have seen some beautiful newspaper buildings. I have also seen a host of mastheads pack up and leave their place of birth for modern and easier-to-maintain premises.

Newsrooms in Canberra, Melbourne and Sydney, with their open landscapes and multi-platform approaches, melding print and online, are world-class environments. Up there with the most impressive is NZME's newsroom in Auckland. This is the home of *The New Zealand Herald* and also houses local radio and a suite of online services. In the middle of the newsroom is a bench where staff congregate for their regular pow-wows. Called the "Bridge", it resembles a surfboard and gives the newsroom a sense of focus.

Plenty of bricks and mortar. Each newsroom has its peculiarities. Each has a story to tell.

Five positive attributes of a modern newsroom

Gizmos and gadgets are prevalent in the modern newsroom. But these are not the things that define an outstanding operation. For me, there are five attributes common to the best newsrooms. They are translatable for any comms environment:

1. an open office landscape
2. face-to-face contact
3. centrally placed management
4. great connectivity
5. a good vibe.

Let's have a look at each of these, and some tips on how you can bring these attributes to your business.

Open office landscape

"It is too costly to restructure." "It will not work with the computer wiring." "The boss is thinking about it."

I have heard most of the excuses about why offices cannot be redesigned.

A floor plan sympathetic to team play is a basic requirement for a DIY Newsroom. People who must collaborate must sit together. A team is not a team if it's in different parts of the building or complex. If a team must be remote, say in different cities, build in processes that ensure everyone is together as much as possible. Skype, Hangout, in-person catch ups. Schedule it. Systemise it.

Should people have permanent office places? Some offices have moved to "hot desking", which is where staff don't have assigned desks and instead move around regularly. This takes the open office landscape to another level. In larger offices hot desking can work, but research from management experts shows employees often resent the constant shifting around. That is offset by the opportunity to mingle with other parts of the business. The point: office design matters.

Face-to-face contact

People can sit together but still not communicate. Sometimes we have to thrust employees together and make them stare eye to eye. That means across a desk from each other, unencumbered – no barriers like corrals or computer monitors getting in the way of conversation. I see plenty of people "working together", but even in an open landscape office you can see invisible lines drawn around desks that mark territory. At times, people will need their own space for private conversations or time out, but this can be catered for with a sensible layout.

Centrally placed management

Lead by example. More and more editors and managers are sitting with their team. Do I need to spell out the benefits? Direct communication of strategy, rapid-fire decision making and implementation, collegiality, team play. When I first became an editor, this was not commonplace. Having a big office and a private conference room represented the stature of the job. I watched with interest, though, as the managing director of one of my clients worked alongside staff each day; the epitome of visible leadership. The opposite is managers who are physically distant, and the business culture pays a price for this.

Great connectivity

I used to have a wooden Dunlop John McEnroe–branded tennis racquet. As much as I loved the touch that racquet gave me, I would not take to the court today with it. There are better options. Whether you run a small communications outfit or a large corporate one, you need the right resources. This relates to your systems – and it's best if they are simple, common, collaborative, connected and in the cloud. I still go into offices where there are restrictions around Wi-Fi. It takes me back to the anally retentive bosses who would not allow journalists to access the internet for fear of them wasting time. Then it became social media.

A communications team needs to be superbly equipped. This means fitting out staff with the right gear so they can do their job as *comm*andos. Consider setting up a mini-studio for video shoots and live streaming. You can easily do that within your marketing budget. And it adds to the …

Good vibe

Newsrooms have a feel. Old timers speak about the pressure chutes that shot pages of copy from department to department – from sub-editors to typesetters or linotypers. I loved the smell of the newsprint and presses that used to waft into the newsroom. And, as I have written already, there is the adrenalin rush and sense of urgency that is palpable in great newsrooms.

You do not hear the clatter of typewriters anymore, and some newsrooms are more library-like than noisy fonts of creativity. But you can create a sense of "this is where stuff happens". Display inspiring company mantras. Set up a computerised screen or use a whiteboard to show tasks for the day and the metrics that matter. If you are not sure what to do, visit a modern newsroom or ask your team what would help increase the buzz. And then fake it until you make it.

Simply the best

The simple things can be the most effective. I saw an amazing turnaround, literally, in one regional newsroom I visited. The team dynamic among the 25 editorial staff was okay, but something was lacking. It was that X-factor: team connection.

The newsroom had moved to a new building and the editorial leaders, while seated together at the top end of the room, were not firing as one. All it took to change that dynamic was a sleight of hand from the editor. First, he brought himself into the hub. Next, he turned the chairs around so staff, who had their backs to each other, now faced each other across a smaller, more intimate round desk.

When I next visited, the level of collaboration had stepped up measurably. Bravo.

CHAPTER 11

CAPTURING THE ESSENCE
OF A NEWSROOM

"The real spiel I have for you is to have a good time while you are in your jobs. Have a good time. The newspaper will be great if you're having a good time."

WASHINGTON POST EDITOR BEN BRADLEE TO GRADUATES
FROM COLUMBIA SCHOOL OF JOURNALISM, 2007

What really makes a newsroom?

A good workplace setup provides us with routine and a sense of community. So what happens when calamity strikes and destroys this? Literally.

Andrew Holden was Editor-in-Chief of *The Press* in Christchurch on 22 February 2011 when a 6.3 earthquake flattened the city. The quake killed 185 people, including a woman at *The Press* who worked on the top floor. The power of networked technology, the smartphone especially, kept Kiwis connected to what was happening at the disaster scene. The physical newsroom was unusable, yet staff quickly set up a DIY newsroom on the village green and later in makeshift facilities.

Here's what Andrew said about this:

Stuart: You lost your newsroom and you were working in the field by and large.

Andrew: On that first day we were, yes.

Stuart: And then you were established in makeshift premises.

Andrew: It was the printing plant which had a café for the printers and we worked out of it, and it had a couple of offices and we worked out of that and gradually, as more and more people returned to the business, we filled up that space quickly, because the company flew in laptops and computers and so we built a porta-cabin complex in the car park of the printing plant which housed, in the end, around 200 people.

Stuart: When we think of newsrooms, we think of buildings, structure, infrastructure. What did your experience following the earthquake tell you?

Andrew: It was cathartic. You don't need any of that stuff.

Stuart: What do you need?

Andrew: There was a famous photograph of us, of the makeshift newsroom in one of the parks on the edge of Christchurch, where our digital editor had grabbed his laptop [just after the quake]. It was the only laptop that we had. Reporters took turns to sit at it, covered in dust, and drops of blood from one of the senior reporters because he'd been wounded in the head – and they took turns to write their stories and send them via email off to the Wellington newsroom. So, a newsroom is a patch of grass and a laptop. But it's a phone as well, you can text it if you must. That porta-cabin there, we had two porta-cabins for the editorial team, the main newsroom had 30, 35 people in it, side-by-side. You put your elbow out, you hit the next person. It got smelly in winter. I used to hold news conferences out around the picnic table next to the barbed-wire fence looking out towards the airport. You can do it anywhere. You don't need the fancy stuff.

One of the things I most admire about the Kiwis is their no-nonsense approach in the most difficult of circumstances. Technology enabled them to continue to do their job. But what stood out was that, other than the bare essentials to file their stories, they did not need the accoutrements we associate with a physical environment. It was the deeper aspects – the systematic way of working, the passion and the camaraderie – that counted in the end. It was the X-factor, the human dimension that allowed them to continue to do their job. Their response to the earthquake left many seasoned journos around the world in awe, and will be talked about within the industry for generations.

The Seven Habits of Highly Effective Newsrooms

This demonstrates that there are Seven Habits of Highly Effective Newsrooms which are more important than the physical environment. How many of these can you tick off in your business?

The seven habits are:

1. Newsrooms are expert storytellers.
2. Newsrooms are organised for chaos.
3. Newsrooms have a sense of urgency.
4. Newsrooms are idea factories.
5. Newsrooms are team-driven and collaborative.
6. Newsrooms change the world.
7. Newsrooms are fun.

Let's consider each of these, and what you can learn from these habits to help your comms team.

Newsrooms are expert storytellers

Data and market research guide the news agenda today. But successful news operations also know intuitively what constitutes a story – they have a nose for news. Even better, they know how to tell the story. Today, a story can be words, video, audio – different media methods that hit different senses.

The lesson for comms teams? Don't rely only on data and market research. Look for the *story*.

Newsrooms are organised for chaos

Newspapers are superb at this. Most of them have spent decades refining the process – systemising the gathering, creating, production and distribution of information. Journalists thrive on the big news, and you never know when something is going to land that requires immediate attention. But it doesn't all come together without a set way of working.

The lesson for comms teams? Be a strategically driven operation where great decisions can be made under pressure. Reflect on a recent epic fail. What let you down? Probably preparation.

Newsrooms have a sense of urgency

Sort of the bleeding obvious, but those in a non-media environment could benefit from instilling a deadline-driven environment. Sure, big projects need time to be formed and delivered. But consider a multi-speed approach, with one layer about getting well-targeted bites of content to specific audiences when it is most beneficial.

The lesson for comms teams? Deliver quick daily wins.

Newsrooms are idea factories

Amazing ideas can come from anywhere – and no one person or one process produces all of them. Believe me, I've been to, or even worse run, news conferences where idea creation was suffocated because the boss thought they knew best. (One of my best front pages was conceived by a photographer in a toilet.) We want our people to be open-minded and see the possibility in a story, not the obstacles.

Similarly, communication teams should scout for the thinking and creativity required.

Newsrooms are team-driven and collaborative

Usually. They can also be competitive in an unhealthy way, and I have seen many a verbal stoush between reporters marking their territory on a story. But they will still defend each other and journalism to the hilt. Senior reporters' generosity to cub reporters knows no bounds as they share tips on interviewing, writing and crafting compelling content. Journalists love kicking the ball around on a good yarn – and when it is published they are the first to congratulate their colleagues. It is worth bottling.

The lesson for comms teams? Always work together and support each other. Intense debates are fine as long as they are not personal and everybody knows you are just trying to hash out the best result.

Newsrooms change the world

Most journalists I know got into the craft to make a difference. And sometimes they can make a big difference with a story. Other times the changes they effect are community based. But good newsrooms have a strong social purpose and a reason for being.

Many brands and companies are looking to make a positive difference too – and they can and should. If your comms messaging can make a heartfelt and authentic connection between your brand and its audiences, magic happens.

Newsrooms are fun

When I walk into a newsroom, it does not take long to work out if it's a happy and healthy one. The best newsrooms are lively, engaged and lack pretension. They are creative and collegial. People are animated and interested in their work. They are not daunted by change but embrace it – because they are accustomed to every day being different. They treat each other as equals.

The lesson for comms teams? A happy, engaged team will lead to great work.

* * *

For all these reasons, newsrooms are intoxicating places to work. Which of these habits would you want to bring to your workplace?

CHAPTER 12

THE GOOD, BAD AND UGLY

"You must unlearn, what you have learned."

YODA

The good

"Best practice" is not a term journalists love. It is business jargon. But it is hard to avoid, because you need to ask, "If I'm going to set up a DIY Newsroom, who does it best?"

In the cut and thrust of a changing media, this is a fraught question. You see it played out at international conferences. One year one media outlet gets all the attention, the next year there is a new kid on the block.

With many years of experience, I do at least have the benefit of being able to give you a 360-degree view of what distinguishes great newsrooms. I can point to three very different examples of news-rooms that tick many boxes. The first is a traditional player in media that has undergone a radical transformation. The second is a big, well-known brand that has created its own newsroom from scratch. The third is an aged-care provider undergoing explosive growth. Let's have a look at these examples to see what you can learn for creating your own DIY Newsroom.

MORE THAN SHINY TOYS: STUFF LIMITED, NEW ZEALAND

This is an organisation that has led from the front while other media organisations have been paralysed by a lack of clarity, vision and courage.

When I began consulting to Stuff (then Fairfax NZ) in late 2014, it was at the crossroads. The company had 70 newspapers across the country, the number one domestic website Stuff.co.nz, and a handful of other interests. It wanted to become a predominantly digital business but was wrestling with the diametrically opposed processes of its newspapers. Digital is go, go, go. Newspapers are about capturing a moment in time, and are deadline and process driven. Streamlining its newspapers was a big and complicated job. But the real mission was to change the culture of the organisation.

Newspapers have engrained cultures. But it is the layers of process that tie them down: production methods, deadlines, the black-and-white nature of how things are done, and a hierarchical organisational structure.

Stuff blew this up. The company rationalised its newspaper holdings. And it radically diversified its business model and created new revenue streams. Stuff did this by starting up businesses or entering into partnerships to sell fibre optic services, health insurance, subscription entertainment and electricity.

What is of interest is how newsroom changes drove the transformation.

Stuff:

- adopted an open and transparent communication process with staff
- equipped employees with the latest technology and ensured it helped them do their jobs – it wasn't just about having the latest gadgets
- used technology to help content creation and delivery become more customer focused and relevant
- moved staff to purpose-built environments or redesigned workplaces to foster collaboration
- encouraged experimentation and celebrated different thinking
- did this at scale and at speed – and did not make many mistakes.

The business did not sugar-coat the need to reduce costs or shrink the print portfolio to survive. But the company never lost sight of its reason for being – helping Kiwi communities to thrive.

ON THE BALL: AFL MEDIA

It's not obvious at first glance to the average Aussie Rules follower, but AFL is a content business. Yes, it's a sport bordering on religion, but it's also a highly profitable entertainment product.

In 2011, former metropolitan journalist Matthew Pinkney began a dream job of building a newsroom from the ground up. The AFL had signed a $100 million, five-year digital rights deal with Australia's number one telecommunications company, Telstra.

The partnering of Australia's number one sport and number one telco made sense from many standpoints. Football brought a huge audience into the sales and marketing funnel for Telstra. At a basic level, it wanted to maximise sales of its AFL Live Pass streaming service, and AFL Media received massive funds to build a future-thinking digital news hub. The goal was to serve sponsors (especially Telstra) and fans, and to elevate the AFL brand.

Where once the AFL relied on external media for its voice – particularly radio, newspapers and TV in football-crazy Melbourne – the league was now making a huge play to control its own product and messaging. Explained Pinkney:

> What Telstra offered as part of that partnership was brilliant infrastructure and technical understanding of how to stream vision onto mobile devices. What they didn't have any idea of was how to build a content offer around that – how to bring an audience in and to get that audience to buy their Live Pass. I got the head of content role and my first job was to create a philosophy for this newsroom.

That meant building a community of content based on the principles and practices of the modern newsroom. It would be the AFL's interface with the public, but for it to become the prime destination for football supporters the content needed to be authoritative, quality journalism.

Today, it is just that. When you walk into AFL Media at the league's headquarters in Docklands, Melbourne, it is like all the best parts of various newsrooms have been pulled together into one place. One part is broadcast oriented, with banks of monitors and production control desks. There is a small studio, and then a newsroom with all the clutter and accoutrements you would see elsewhere.

AFL Media is a fully fledged modern newsroom operation of 120 staff, about 40 of whom work directly on content. Until recently, this included a publishing arm that produced magazines, a stats-packed Season Guide, and a host of other super-quality publications. There is a dedicated social media team of four who feed Facebook, Snapchat and other platforms, keeping up the conversation and engagement with audiences across the globe. But most journalists, positioned across every football state, work across platforms.

Pinkney is modest about what he created, but under his strategic direction AFL Media has blossomed into a newsroom as prolific and proactive as most traditional newsrooms. During the footy season, afl.com.au regularly rates as the number one sports website in the country.

What AFL Media shows is that the principles and practices of a DIY Newsroom can be applied for superb impact in the non-media sector. In the AFL's case, it built a new communications enterprise from the base up, with no resemblance to the stock-standard external public relations units you normally see in the corporate world.

Few companies have the AFL's level of resources. But in microcosm you can achieve similar results.

DIY NEWSROOM SUCCESS: RYMAN HEALTHCARE, NEW ZEALAND AND AUSTRALIA

How do you communicate effectively in one of the fastest growing sectors in the world? Where new communities are created every year and residents yearn for connection? Answer: build your own newsroom.

Ryman has constructed and runs 32 retirement villages, predominantly in New Zealand, and is expanding into Australia. At last count, it had more than a dozen other villages on the drawing board. Those villages are part of the solution to the greatest demographic change the world has seen: a rapidly ageing population.

For an organisation of such considerable scale like Ryman – 5000 staff, 10,800 residents and thousands of other contractors and suppliers spread over 40 locations – going the DIY route for communications sounds decidedly non-corporate. But it is deliberately home-based for the best business and marketing reasons.

When David King began as corporate affairs manager with Ryman Healthcare in 2013, he was a one-man band, faced with the immediate and daunting challenge of how best to keep the company's growing community informed.

Since then, David, a former business reporter and editorial manager, has built his own community – a modest DIY Newsroom of five that produces a steady stream of publications, social media posts and video, and serves the wider communication and PR needs of the business.

Developing a DIY Newsroom happened more organically than anything – but the outcomes have been as impressive as you would find from any marketing outfit.

A microcosm of Ryman, the comms team is geographically spread, David based in Christchurch and his staff otherwise spread through New Zealand and now in Melbourne.

The team continues to work in tandem with the marketing team to produce hard-copy newsletters and other shareholder and staff magazines. In total, that's some 140 different publications a year – an output akin to many small community newspaper operations.

Ryman has judiciously added social and digital media to its media mix to serve key audiences: residents, their extended families and the huge base of workers.

Each village has its own Facebook page – and the comms team has started running Facebook workshops to help residents. The comms team keeps pages fresh with regular new content. The Ryman website is the mothership or repository for a lot of content, a touchpoint for visitors and prospective families. Internally, staff use Yammer to share stories and for messaging. Ryman also tells its story over LinkedIn to promote careers in aged care. As well, the comms team has started live streaming community events across social media.

Ryman uses Twitter sparingly and Instagram for recruitment – it is careful about getting the right fit for an already stretched small team. But the organisation has embraced the power of video – and sending it viral.

If you search YouTube you will find yourself shuffling your shoes to Ryman's clever spoof of Pharrell Williams's *Happy* and elderly residents twerking to Taylor Swift's *Shake It Off*. Each video has recorded some nine million views. These break stereotypes, are great subliminal marketing, but were also just damn fun for residents to make.

The villages are fertile grounds for a comms team with a nose for news. "Four of us are journalists. The other is a photographer who can write," David said. "We took those skills and created our own community of news. We have great stories to tell – we have 100-year-olds who go paragliding."

"We have become a one-stop shop for communications and PR and an important resource for our marketing team. And we have the newsroom skills of being able to write, take pictures, package stories and get information out quickly."

Each Anzac Day, Ryman publishes a souvenir publication that profiles the service of veterans living at the village, stories that might otherwise not be told.

Ryman's newsroom has contributed to the resounding goodwill around the organisation. It also tracks success in the usual way – mentions, audience engagement and the like.

It is not all happy hours in aged care, though. The sector can be risky business, and the comms teams has to be on its toes. When needed, David and his staff provide crisis comms or other advice to the executive.

"The hardest thing is keeping up with where the audience is going to next," David said. "You need people with skills and who are savvy and looking at what to do next. Facebook is always changing its rules and audiences change too. We also have to be careful about the privacy of residents and moderate comments.

"The safest and easiest thing might be to just put out print as we used to do. But that is not how people want to communicate with us – they want to be engaged 24–7."

Going DIY is more economical than going the agency route. It has also been the perfect fit for the Ryman way, where it seems that if it's worth doing properly it's worth doing yourself.

"Our company is DIY in many ways. That suits us because we have a lot of expertise inside and this suits our culture," explained David. "We have our own architects, apprentices and nurses – and we do not outsource a lot. We like to learn things ourselves, so we can understand and then have the control. This is opposite to the ethos of a lot of companies, I know, but it has meant we have been able to build up a massive trust factor."

The bad and the ugly

Not all newsrooms are high-performing, well-adjusted operations like Stuff, AFL Media and Ryman. I have seen some shockers (buy me a beer for names). To be fair, just as no one newsroom does all things superbly, no one newsroom gets it wrong all the time. But, let me group the bad and the ugly into a neat, not-so-fabulous five, so you can also see what *not* to do:

1. The Sausage Factory.
2. The Conflict Zone.
3. The JJ Jameson Newsroom.
4. The Zombie Newsroom.
5. The Buttoned-down Newsroom.

Let's take a look.

The Sausage Factory

This is the newsroom that just goes through the motions. They work the way they worked 10 years ago, with some minor adjustments, pumping out a predictable digest of news and information – enough volume to fill air time, social channels and the pre-requisite number of column centimetres. They are moribund and losing audience, who are dying of boredom or, as in the case of some newspapers, actually dying.

The Conflict Zone

Newsrooms are high-octane environments. Sometimes this tips over into brutal combat and the bar on behaviour drops to a horrendous low. These newsrooms are not a fun place to work. Only a generation ago it was standard operating practice for editors to bawl out staff. I know of one editor who threw a phone at a journalist, hitting him in the head. Women were subjected to routine sexism in and out of the office. I worked in one newsroom where it was not uncommon for there to be screaming matches between staff. Nothing cool about this.

The JJ Jameson Newsroom

Any self-respecting superhero series like Spiderman needs a *Daily Bugle*. Editor John Jonah Jameson is the personification of the personality-driven and agenda-driven newsroom. Us newspaper romantics love this stuff. JJ lives, breathes and eats newspapers. Unfortunately, there is a dark side to such newsrooms. It is all about the narcissistic boss and his take-no-prisoners approach for sales.

The Zombie Newsroom

At the other end of the spectrum are the walking-dead newsrooms. They have no pulse. They only survive by sucking off the life-force provided by a tolerant and uninterested management. Everything they do is lifeless. The content they produce is predictable – bland, boring and banal. They have an uncanny ability to kill any story with potential with their naysaying and pessimism. They are leaderless, lacklustre and lame.

The Buttoned-down Newsroom

This newsroom has a good dose of sausage making. But it is mainly characterised by its hierarchical and cautious nature. Creative thought is frowned upon. There is a regimented way of doing things, the antithesis of what is required in today's information-driven economy. Their physical environment is more akin to a library than a news hub.

* * *

Companies today are big on designing a workplace that reflects their wider values and culture. In reality, managers are the ones who drive the operational feel of a workplace. How would you describe yours? Ask yourself and those around you what your comms office should be like. How can you effect the changes required?

PART IV

THE DIY
JOURNALIST

CHAPTER 13

A WALKING, TALKING, ONE-PERSON NEWSROOM

"Once writing has become your major vice and greatest pleasure only death can stop it."

AMERICAN NOVELIST ERNEST HEMINGWAY (1899–1961)

A long time ago, in a galaxy far, far away ...

When I began in journalism on a small country newspaper I had part of a journalism degree, a small portable typewriter, a notebook and pencils, dodgy shorthand and a camera I did not know how to use. I had enthusiasm, confidence, permed peroxide hair (hey, it was the '80s) and a passion to change the world.

I told my stories in a linear and traditional way. I would bang out each new paragraph on a separate piece of copy paper, it would be marked up by the editor for news English, grammar and with typographical instructions. My typewritten stories would be typeset and galleys of bromides produced. Compositors would slice these up with the sharpest of knives and glue them onto the columns of pages.

I took all the photos for the paper. The film would be developed, the editor would circle the photos he wanted on a proof sheet. Those photos would be printed, sized with a protractor-like wheel and sent out to be made into a bromide, cut to shape and composited onto the page with the matching story.

The page would "go to camera", a printing plate was made, plates were organised on the press, the newsprint was loaded and the press would roar into action.

This was not the entirety of the process – but you can see the production of the news was as big a deal as gathering it. While the editor and I comprised the news department, dozens of other people were involved in the production process to get our newspaper to readers. And similar labour-intensive production processes existed for radio and TV.

That was then, this is now – and we will never see anything like that again. I loved the smell of newsprint that permeated the entire building. But, for all the romance of print in its halcyon times, how I would have killed for the tools of today to tell my stories.

Being a cyber-journalist

What more could the communications professional of today want? They have the skills and the smarts. They have a huge arsenal of storytelling devices. They have totally accessible, often free, media platforms. They do not need multi-million-dollar television and radio studios, back-breaking equipment, licences, or printing presses.

Today, anyone who wants to engage in storytelling, or just share rubbish, can do so at low to no cost. Today, everyone is a publisher. Today, you can be a walking, talking, sharing, videoing, one-person newsroom – a DIY journalist. For businesses, that means unprecedented possibilities for cementing relationships with existing clients and audiences. But the real opportunity is reaching new clients and new audiences – and being better than your competitors.

While a DIY journalist has incredible mobility and is multi-skilled, they still need to operate in a structured environment to be effective. This is vital for business leaders to understand. Great content and great outcomes do not just happen. This needs to be orchestrated.

A big part of that is recruiting the right people with the right set of personal attributes for the DIY Newsroom.

Let's take a look …

12 qualities of a crack *comm*ando

As an editor, I expected my reporters to bring their A-game to the office every day. There could be no such thing as a bad day. The same applies to the DIY journalist. As *comm*andos, they need to be all-terrain operators – of a sturdy and robust nature.

For me, there are a dozen personal traits common to top journalists:

1. **Get-up-and-go:** Journalists are ambitious, competitive and highly motivated. You want staff champing at the bit to chase that story.

2. **Curiosity:** About what makes people tick. About life.

3. **Tech smart:** In flat-pack land you have to be able to handle an Allen key. In the DIY Newsroom you need to be able to shoot and upload a video and work out how to use myriad apps on a smartphone.

4. **Adaptability:** To achieve the above. Also, to sustain the waves of change that will continue to hit communications. As we learned with Darwin's survival of the fittest, it is not the strong who emerge to fight another day but those most able to adapt.

5. **Street smart:** The sixth sense that is hard to define, but is gold when you find it.

6. **Calm under fire:** When others lose their heads, you want people who can get on with the task at hand.

7. **Quick smart:** Being first does matter. You want people who can clinically and quickly punch through priorities.

8. **Eye for detail:** Which does not go with the above, generally – but you want both regardless. If you post content quickly and often and it is second rate, your brand will be punished and you will be reputationally exposed.

9. **Challenging:** Not in a pain-in-the-ass way, but someone who has the audacity and confidence to tell you how it is.

10. **Communicative:** Of course.

11. **Ethical:** People who do what is right – not just what is easy or comfortable.

12. **Humanitarian:** People who treat others as they would want to be treated – known variously as the Golden Rule or the "no dickheads policy".

Excellent writing and communication skills are a given.

If you have the resources, it's great to have a team of people who complement each other – a good utility player you can move around the ground depending on the day, a dead-eye Dick who never misses when lined up in front of goal, a defender who can tie down the opposition.

As an editor, I found there were generally three classes of reporter:

- the reporter who could "get" any story but might struggle to write it
- the reporter who could light a fire with their beautiful prose but the story might lack the fundamentals
- that rarest of gems who could do both.

In big newsrooms that I ran, you could afford to have journalists who had specialist rounds or brought a unique but perhaps solitary dimension to the business. In the communications environment of today, that is impractical. In a DIY Newsroom, journalists must be ambidextrous and utilitarian. And their eyes must be on the prize: to build communities of interest by using the tools at their disposal for powerful and engaging storytelling.

All in a day's work

Journalists love the variety of their job. They get new assignments each day, explore exciting places, interview fascinating people and find themselves at the centre of the action.

DIY journalists can do this too – and add zing with all that modern storytelling methods bring. A typical day could include:

1. researching, creating, packaging and distributing fascinating content that captures people's attention
2. mastering social media platforms

3. hosting live streams

4. producing and presenting webinars and podcasts

5. running public events

6. organising marketing campaigns with a difference

7. using the latest technology and apps to create, edit and deliver professional video that becomes a talking point

8. learning new stuff

9. tracking and recording community engagement with your brand – and reporting that with a smile to the boss.

If that does not make for a stimulating job, then I have nothing else to offer. Because there has never been a better time to be a communicator, and never been a better time to go DIY.

CHAPTER 14

TAILORING YOUR MESSAGE TO YOUR AUDIENCE

"Think Different."

APPLE ADVERTISEMENT, 1977

Each DIY Newsroom will have its own character and field of activity. It could be a newsroom for a financial institution, local government, national sports body, college or humanitarian cause.

Even as the foundations are being laid, a DIY Newsroom or DIY Journalist can:

- tailor coverage to a targeted audience
- provide relevant and engaging content
- deliver content in the form the audience wants it
- create and expand communities of interest around what you do
- track performance and put in a process of continual improvement
- boost your brand and reputation
- generate a stack of fun.

Whatever the industry, field of activity or cause, each newsroom will have its own audiences and mission.

Many local governments would benefit greatly from developing a DIY Newsroom. As an example of how to tailor your message to your audience, let's have a look at what local governments could do to improve their communication.

Stop hiding your light

Local government is the poster child for an organisation hiding its light under a bushel – and it's time for it to shine.

Many residents and ratepayers rate their councils lowly. We know that because even the councils say it. I have checked in on some of the community engagement statistics for various councils, and there is nothing to write home about.

I think about the relationship with my council and often wonder what goes on at city hall. How does the council and its managers view the role of communications?

Like many other councils, mine is doing a better job on social media than it did a couple of years ago. It posts more to Facebook, occasionally tweets when the local pool is closed, which is helpful, live streams council meetings, and is starting to produce good video. But I do not recall ever receiving an email update from the council or any return correspondence when I have submitted feedback. I do not receive a community newsletter, and all that seems to lob in the letterbox is the quarterly rates notice.

I am not a prolific user of the council's services, but as a former local editor I think I appreciate the sorts of activities the council is involved in. But I lament: why isn't the council telling me its story? The council must be doing a whole stack of cool and innovative stuff. The council must be providing an array of services that could help me and others plug in to our communities.

To me, this seems to be an incredible lost opportunity. And I know my council is no different from many other local governments that have hundreds of touchpoints with residents but do not get the recognition for the great work they do – and this is the same for many organisations in other fields.

The Seven Signs of Civic Unrest

In the case of local government, there are some special circumstances. I call them the Seven Signs of Civic Unrest:

1. **Lack of strategic vision:** Some councils are working in the old way and fail to see how introducing a strategic communications framework can springboard them into new areas of engagement.

2. **Lack of resources:** This is often quoted to me as a reason why organisations cannot more proactively promote themselves. But most local councils have at least a handful of people in marketing and comms who can be marshalled around any activity if prioritised.

3. **Council bashing:** It is a national sport. We all have gripes about our council. And some administrations, when under siege, think no news is good news. Councils can also get locked in a negative zone, constantly working to counter the flak or smooth over the latest controversy.

4. **Internal politics and bureaucracy:** Many council comms professionals totally get the newsroom concept, having worked for local media. But mayors, general managers and other executives can suck the life out of a good idea. They might be conservative and lack a spirit of adventure. Or they are controlling. Or council division and personality politics make proactive communications like walking a high wire.

5. **Media fragmentation:** Council teams tell me they find it hard to get their messages out through local media today because the local newsroom is stretched, regularly makes mistakes or is adversarial.

6. **General cynicism about authority:** The Edelman Trust Barometer shows our distrust of traditional institutions is rising.

7. **Wariness about social media:** Moderating the community conversation is a minefield for local councils who are easy prey for critics and naysayers. It is one of the reasons why council hierarchies wince when comms teams encourage them to go forth and multiply their messages. They see it as dangerous to engage.

If the status quo is not reaping the results you seek, what is the antidote? Surely it's not to keep doing the same thing. It is time to change things up.

Creating the virtual village square

Most of the council comms people I know have the skills and the nous to create what I call the virtual village square and to become the primary destination for local information. Councils can reclaim their historic place as the town square for the community conversation instead of just being seen as maintaining some of our essential services like local roads and collecting the rubbish.

Those working in or responsible for communications are already incentivised around the notion because their KPIs are to:

- increase community engagement and goodwill (and do so measurably)
- reach as extensively across the constituency as possible with accurate and helpful information
- cast the council and staff in the best light possible
- deal effectively with complaints and the burning issues of the day
- liaise with external stakeholders – such as local media and community representatives – and internal stakeholders for positive results.

Of course, a DIY council newsroom cannot be entirely "independent". We still need strong independent journalism to hold our authorities to account. Sadly, the closure of many local papers and their offices has meant communities now lack that – and local media does not have the resources to cover as many events and areas as it did.

For their part, councils can fill part of the void by doing a better job at promoting what is going on in their communities and by providing an open forum for community discussion. This is an unprecedented opportunity because councils have the tools and platforms to reach all residents.

Creating micro-communities

Local government provides and supports an amazing array of services: children's activities, public parks, arts activities, libraries – far more than just the proverbial roads, rates and rubbish. These are the very topic areas around which the council can build micro-communities.

I will explain in more detail about the network of channels councils can use and how to sustain this, but I am guessing you know most of them already.

Each city has its own character and own communities of interest. My municipality has more than a dozen patrolled beaches. There's lots of information that beachgoers could benefit from, and lots of opportunities to engage with them in a positive manner through council communications.

Another community would be around public parks and gardens. I lived in the historic city of Ballarat for many years. It is blessed with a beautiful environment, and residents are garden proud. What sort of information could the city provide here? The city also had an active arts community.

I ran several local newspapers in inner-suburban Melbourne where heritage was an issue. That represents another community of interest. Each municipality has its own suburbs with their own interests, events and character. Again, micro-communities.

As well, newsrooms are good at identifying and swarming on issues of the day, which in a council context can galvanise groups of people to create healthier results for the community. On some issues, a council newsroom may want to stay neutral. But even if an issue is one that polarises the community, the council comms team could do much to enrich the public conversation and build engagement and understanding.

For example, what might this look like in the case of whether dogs should be allowed on beaches? The council could:

1. outline "for" and "against" arguments on the council website

2. provide a short video of resident vox pops on the issue and share across social media

3. run a community poll

4. produce a podcast with an independent expert who has had to contend with competing views

5. use the council's email database to update residents with a special "dog" edition

6. live stream the council debate

7. provide a series of factoids on dogs and the council's animal services to share across the council's various channels.

All or none of these could work, the point being to think and act like a newsroom; that is, in a strategic manner. These would be some of the angles an editor would have a news team chase.

When I spoke to a local government conference, a comms professional from Port Adelaide shared how he was starting to produce video on basic council services. He profiled the workers who filled the potholes in the city's roads. Gold. It can be as simple as that. And, like with most good stories, they are about people.

Creating a community around content is applicable in all sectors, not just local government. The principles of providing quality storytelling to distinct audiences are just as relevant whether you are trying to maximise engagement as a big company or as a small not-for-profit.

All about results

By putting the basics in, a whole lot of good stuff starts to happen:

- better community engagement, which makes for more informed decision-making (decisions that have a real community mandate and that stick)

- you become a respected information destination

99

- you get a shot of reputation inoculation – credit in the bank for when the bad times inevitably arise
- you reposition yourself as a thought leader in the sector, not merely a provider of services
- you are recognised for what you do.

Opening up a two-way conversation with audiences requires a heightened level of monitoring, curating and responding to people.

Why would the council CEO or mayor or the boss of any organisation want to expose themselves to debate and the possibility of criticism? Aside from the above, the WIIFM (what's in it for me?) factor must surely be convincing. As community engagement levels rise, the council and its managers stand out. Councillors' political stocks increase. The community better understands and appreciates the services on offer. There is an improved sense of belonging and sense of value for money. And for those driving the comms? Making the boss look like a rock star is good for the communicator and their career.

The secret to success, though, lies in doing this in a simple, strategic and sustainable way.

PART V

THE SMART WAY™

CHAPTER 15

THE SMART STEPS TO KILLER COMMS

*"There's a force in the universe that makes things happen.
And all you have to do is get in touch with it, stop thinking,
let things happen, and be the ball."*

TY WEBB, CHEVY CHASE'S CHARACTER IN
THE 1980 CLASSIC GOLF COMEDY *CADDY SHACK*

A new communications approach

In my travels, in the research for this book, as I speak at conferences, work with clients and consult on projects, I see organisations and individuals doing amazing things with their communications.

I marvel at how they are creatively using video and social media to get their message out. How they reach thousands of prospects through email marketing. And how community engagement has become a more targeted science.

Unfortunately, these activities often have little context in an organisation's greater mission.

My SMART Way™ is the secret sauce that brings together each phase and aspect of modern communications, providing an integrated approach. SMART is the product of my experience across more than 30 years in traditional and new media. I am passionate about helping organisations to shine, but willing this to happen is not enough. That's why I developed the SMART methodology, to systemise best practice.

SMART stands for **S**trategy, **M**edia, **A**uthenticity, **R**esults and **T**eam – the five steps to simple, strategic, successful and sustainable communications. It is designed as an easy-to-remember acronym. SMART begins with the premise that unless you work for the CIA or MI5, being recognised for what you do is a good thing.

The five SMART steps

We all lead busy lives and, as such, this system will help you target what is not working for you. Not sure what to prioritise (Results)? How can we sustain what we do – we only have a small crew (Team)? Is this viral campaign true to our brand (Authenticity)? What are we aiming to do in the first place (Strategy)?

You might apply all of the five SMART steps chronologically, for it does present a logical path. But you may find you already have a sound comms strategy in place and are happy with your network of media channels, so you can jump ahead. Or you may have the logistics of social media scheduling all sorted but need to go back and review your plan.

In short, it is the sum of the five parts of SMART that will allow you to fully exploit the benefits of a DIY Newsroom – and it constitutes a communications approach fit for our times.

Let's look at each step.

Strategy

Strategy starts with a forensic examination of your current state: strengths, obstacles, mistakes and resources. Unpacking your problems can be confronting, confounding, enlightening and liberating. We then go about building the perfect plan for you to become an influencer and leader in your sector.

Elements I cover include:

- understanding what having a strategy really means – and defining what it looks like
- how to conduct a comms health check
- how to conduct a content audit
- identifying your audiences and content communities
- moving from strategy to action.

Media

Modern marketers typically jump to the shiny new objects. Snapchat, Weibo, Periscope, Facebook. You want to control your content? You need to control your platforms and develop a content ecosystem and delivery schedule that is simple and sustainable. I explain how to choose and deploy the right weapons of mass communication.

This is where the action and fun starts. Elements I cover include:

- creating content communities
- how to form a content recipe
- packaging content
- forming your media ecosystem (your channels)
- why print still matters
- how best to distribute content.

Authenticity

To be the real deal, a DIY Newsroom needs soul. Authenticity is more than a buzzword. It is of rising value and has an impact on how you go about communicating internally and externally. One of the aspects that distinguishes extraordinary companies from the ordinary ones is making a heartfelt connection with audiences by articulating a deeper purpose.

In this section, I cover:

- Trump, fake news and disruption
- how to design a communications code of ethics
- what a values-driven newsroom looks like.

Results

You want a return on your communications. You want recognition. You want results. You want to elevate yourself above the vanity game – that quick dopamine shot – of likes and shares. You want results that translate to increased sales and profits, and reputational enhancement.

Here I provide you with:

- a template to construct metrics that measure the real return on investment
- specifications for building your DIY Newsroom
- a steer on the tools and technology, including mobile journalism, that will drive high performance.

Team

People power is your X-factor. Your employees will lead your communications revolution. But you will only become a leader in your sector if you successfully inspire, mobilise and lead your people. If you are confused, overwhelmed and disappointed by the results of your current communications then that indicates you need to rethink your team approach.

I show you:

- how to reset your human resources
- a best-practice newsroom org structure
- why good workflow is critical to success
- the essential habits of highly effective teams.

All good? Let's start SMART.

FIVE STEPS TO SMART COMMUNICATIONS

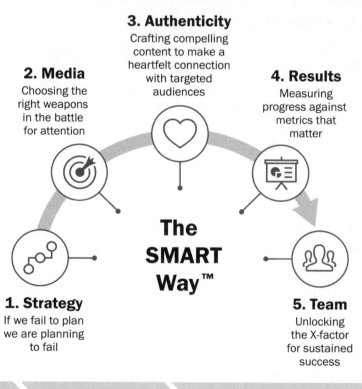

3. Authenticity
Crafting compelling content to make a heartfelt connection with targeted audiences

2. Media
Choosing the right weapons in the battle for attention

4. Results
Measuring progress against metrics that matter

The SMART Way™

1. Strategy
If we fail to plan we are planning to fail

5. Team
Unlocking the X-factor for sustained success

SMART PATH From ... lacking results and not knowing how to make change   To ... communicating with purpose, making change and getting the recognition you deserve

CHAPTER 16

STRATEGY

"If you have a problem that can be fixed, then there is no use in worrying. If you have a problem that cannot be fixed, then there is no use in worrying."

BUDDHIST PROVERB

Why we need strategy

In modern marketing and communications, we are told to think and act like entrepreneurs. This means thinking quick, being "agile" and planning for the short term. This is useful.

But, without a roadmap showing the bigger picture, we are bound to get lost, waste time and forget what the journey was about in the first place. I am a strong believer that nine-tenths of success is in the planning. It is why we should spend considerable time in this zone, time that will save us energy later.

John P. Kotter, a Harvard professor and regarded as a leading authority on change management, cites eight mistakes companies make with their transformation programs. These are:

1. allowing too much complacency

2. failing to create a sufficiently powerful guiding coalition

3. underestimating the power of vision

4. under-communicating the vision by a factor of 10 (or 100, or even 1000)

5. permitting obstacles to block the new vision

6. failing to create short-term wins

7. declaring victory too soon

8. neglecting to anchor changes firmly in the corporate culture.

All of these can be routed back to a failure to plan.

If we fail to plan, we plan to fail

When I survey various industries, I'm unsurprised when organisations confess they have strategies that are deficient or outdated. And some have no strategy at all, or they have marketing plans but nothing deeper.

Building strategy can be, but should not be, a complicated process. Discussing strategic aims opens up debate about issues some people would prefer not discussed. And there are plenty of other reasons to avoid developing strategy. These include protestations such as…

- **We do not need one:** We've been successful in the past. Strategy is business mumbo-jumbo.
- **We do not have the time:** Hey, we're running a business here.
- **We do not have the skills:** What is involved with developing a strategy? Who is going to do this? Do we need to pay for consultants?

Buddha in the boardroom

A short drive from where I lived was a Buddhist temple. I am not a Zen sort of guy, but I loved taking my kids there for a moment of serenity. On the way into the temple, along the narrow cobblestone paths through manicured gardens, were small statues with Buddhist inscriptions. One of them was the proverb at the start of this chapter. It is similar to the Serenity Prayer, written by American theologian Reinhold Niebuhr:

> God, grant me the serenity to accept the things I cannot change.
> Courage to change the things I can.
> And wisdom to know the difference.

This is sage advice for our personal lives. It applies equally to making change at a professional level.

If there was a "business Buddha", I think he would have us apply calm to the boardroom table by asking us to control what we can and acknowledge and let go of what we cannot.

What makes great strategy?

Writing strategy is an art in distilling the complex to the simple.

In the case of an overall business plan, a good strategy constitutes breaking down what a business does, understanding the drivers in the industry, establishing the core values and objectives of the organisation, and setting out a roadmap to success. This needs to be summarised, documented and communicated – while ensuring those affected come along for the ride. Fundamentally, great strategy is about clever storytelling, and that applies whether it is a governing blueprint or a content plan.

Hundreds of books have been written about strategy, but few set out a best-practice template for what a strategy ought to look like. I have my way and methodology. As you build your DIY Newsroom, you will have yours. Your strategy could be a:

- written report
- presentation/slide-deck
- email
- standalone website, web page or content formed on a digital platform
- formal printed document
- infographic
- combination of the above.

Strategy is not just "thinking". It needs to be captured somehow and shared with others. So, it is not nebulous.

In forming your strategy, I urge you to:

1. Keep it simple so it can be easily absorbed. You might have a lot of detail that sits in the background, but think "executive summary".
2. Communicate it visually where you can with a handful of well-constructed images, charts and statements.
3. Contextualise it within your business framework. How does your communications strategy relate to the rest of your business?

4. Package it. Tie it up in a box with a ribbon on top – figuratively, that is. It will be part of your content collateral, used internally and maybe externally. Make it look smart.

5. Get excited. Be passionate about how your new communications plan will reinvigorate your business and the recognition your products, services and people will receive because of that. Talk about that regularly. Everyone should speak from the same script.

In the complex world of communications, a good strategy will be your ballast.

How to create your strategy

Developing strategy need not be costly or cumbersome. It will take time, but it need not be a laborious process – and as you collaborate with others, it can reignite passions about your business mission. It can even be fun.

If you are planning any change within your business, involving those who will be impacted – and have to implement what is agreed – is part of the starting criteria.

I follow this process:

- **Informal discussion:** What is the problem we are trying to solve? What has been tried before? What would we like to achieve?

- **Discovery session:** This is a brainstorm, working with key players within the business, getting a sense of how they operate, their challenges and expectations, and the opportunities. It is a precursor to ...

- **Communications review:** The full-blown, under-the-hood investigation – and where a strategy is formed. The review leads to a series of recommendations for the business to consider. The pointy end might be a one-page overview of how change would occur; for example, three stages with timings and the expected outcomes for each phase.

- **Implementation:** Putting the above into action.
- **Reinforcement and review:** Routinely overlooked, but smart organisations circle back to lock in achievements and make improvements.

Your communications health check

"Simple can be harder than complex: You have to work hard to get your thinking clean to make it simple. But it's worth it in the end because once you get there, you can move mountains."

APPLE ICON STEVE JOBS

I have an amazing doctor. He is terrific at his job, knows my history, communicates simply and, most importantly, I have confidence in the way he practises medicine. This is exactly what you want when it comes to your health.

When feeling the pulse of your business, you similarly want a no-nonsense, fact-based method that gives you an honest appraisal. Nothing beats a clinical, intricate look-see.

There are some essential aspects of a health check when it comes to your communications. But, like a doctor ordering tests, we need an appreciation of how deep a dive is required. On deciding this, you can choose from a range of diagnostics. When I go into a business, I start with the basics and keep drilling from there. The information I uncover and examine includes:

- business basics (organisational mission, strategic papers, codes of conduct, policies)
- heritage (company story, results)
- market characteristics (demographics, catchment area, market size)

- products and platforms (traditional and new media communication channels used – internal and external)
- existing communication collateral (content schedule and strategy, digital schedule and strategy, style guides, user guides)
- human resources (organisational structure, communications team, job descriptions, fan base, volunteers, administrative support)
- financials (communications budget, staff establishment)
- content (existing content recipe, design and style standards)
- content management (commissioning processes, policies or strategies)
- "newsroom" (physical configuration and set up of comms office, seating plan, production and editing facilities, digital dashboards, TV feeds, meeting rooms)
- newsroom equipment (smartphones, computers and other tech, photo and video equipment, transport, admin facilities)
- technology (content platform, Wi-Fi access, community Wi-Fi, office software, other software, platforms and digital tools, video conferencing)
- learning and development (training provided, trainers, appraisal and coaching)
- website (separate audit)
- social media (separate audit)
- content workflow (any engrained way of working, deadlines, scheduling)
- internal communications (updates, staff access to company information, meetings, inductions, rewards and celebration, social events)
- community (sponsorship, community events, level of interaction, customer satisfaction)
- competition (platforms, results, strategies).

This constitutes an excellent sweep of the state of comms, and can form the basis of your own internal comms audit. You could do this on a spreadsheet. For some clients I get them to fill in an online form; that is, I make it self-serve so it saves everyone time and money. You could use a project tool.

Companies spend a lot of money on consultants to gather such information. Doing it yourself from the above list may save you some time, but there is also merit in having an independent auditor. But, as long as you have thought about the process, there is no reason why someone in your organisation could not do this.

With this information in hand, you have a baseline to review your communications against. What do you see? What stands out for change? What needs investigation? From here, you will see if you need first aid or major surgery.

Conducting a content audit

While the health check will inform your overall communications plan, special attention must be paid to what you are primarily there to produce: content. You have heard that content is king. In my mind, it forms the rest of the royal family too.

I see top-line communicators and CEOs break into a sweat when I start talking content plans. As a journalist, content is second nature to me. But businesses struggle with content – it says more work to them, and it may not be their strong suit. An Australian Sensis study found that what most stressed marketers was how to generate content ideas and convert them to stories.

All organisations produce a wealth of content – they just don't know it. The purpose of the content audit is to take a little time to evaluate what they do produce and to bottle it. Without fail, clients are amazed when we go through the process. And we do not have to dig deep to find gold.

I once conducted a communications review for a local church. Our aim was to better position the church in the local community through a SMART approach. The discovery process revealed an active church ecosystem that extended well beyond Sunday services. The church ran almost a dozen distinct groups of activities, including a men's shed, children's playgroup, pre-loved goods shop, and English classes for migrants. The outside world knew next to nothing about any of this. What an opportunity.

The church ran a virtually "invisible" website, used Facebook in a limited fashion and produced a weekly newsletter. However, it had an array of content that could be repurposed. Why couldn't a sermon on Sunday be reused as a blog? Or what a guest speaker said at the men's breakfast posted to Facebook? A new community service provided by the church described in a webinar series?

I worked with another client, a large independent school of more than 3000 students, where we identified 60 different types of content. Not stories, not communication channels but categories of content: headmasters' blog, individual achievements of students, messaging on the college's electronic display boards, concert performances and other events, alumni activities and more. Identifying this information allowed us to recalibrate the communications strategy and to think how to best distribute each piece of content.

Again, a brainstorm of people from across the business can identify content now being produced. Like the health check, a content audit need not be anything more than a spreadsheet. With this information in hand, you can analyse where there are gaps. What opportunities are you missing? What content should you be producing? What content would your market and audiences benefit from?

A content audit can be done as part of the health check, and certainly early on as part of the discovery process. You could do it in one morning and get others involved to comment and review before presenting to your Chief Content Officer (the comms manager?).

When you have mapped your existing and planned content and identified the areas you need to focus on, you will be able to match each type of content with the relevant communication channels (for example, Facebook, your website, a brochure) and type of media (for example, video, text).

Much of what you do will be determined by who you are trying to reach. Your audience. Or, should I say, *audiences*.

Identifying audiences

Having an intimate understanding of your target market is Business 101. However, companies often make the mistake of spraying as many people as possible with their communications.

This is apparent with email marketing. I'm a big fan of email newsletters. I advise using direct email as a primary channel for many companies. However, the emails need to be targeted – you want people to opt in because they find value in your content. Don't spam them so you can add numbers to your distribution lists. Quality, not quantity, is what counts in the Attention Economy.

Identifying audiences is a critical component of the SMART content code, where the aim is to distribute compelling and relevant content to the right audiences, using the most appropriate media, at the best time and via the right channel for maximum return.

Working with the Melbourne college I mentioned before, we identified 16 audiences. Remember, this was a large enterprise of hundreds of staff, thousands of students and an extended community of hundreds of thousands of people. Audiences included:

- the entire college community
- past and current students
- staff
- prospective families

- local residents
- various campuses and activities
- local businesses
- government
- education authorities
- a burgeoning international student body.

Was there any one piece of content or communication we would send to everyone? Highly unlikely.

The audience ID for your business starts with a brainstorm. Who do you reach now? Who do you want to reach? Are there influencers who can promote your brand? List your audiences in a spreadsheet or document, and incorporate this information in your content plan. Your content plan or map would then show:

- categories of content you produce
- applicable audiences
- best channel/s to use considering those audiences
- types of media to deploy.

You do not want the process to become "paralysis by analysis", but I find applying a methodology is useful until it becomes second nature.

Like the other strategic processes mentioned above, an audience ID need take no more than a couple of hours with the right people in the room. Have a review process and build it into your strategy, so your content can be guided to its target like a missile.

How many audience segments is reasonable? This is up to you. You might have half-a-dozen key audiences and then sub-segments.

Once your DIY Newsroom is up and running, hold regular strategic reviews to keep what you do fresh and targeted at the right people.

Turning strategy into action

At some point you have to take the game plan onto the ground. This does not always go smoothly.

I was only a boy at the time, but I love the folklore that has evolved around the 1975 Victorian Football League grand final between my team, Hawthorn, and their arch nemesis of the time, North Melbourne. With the Hawks down 20 points, legendary coach John Kennedy implored his players: "Do. Don't think … don't hope. Do. At least you can come off and say, 'I did this, I shepherded, I played on. At least I did something for the sake of the side". Speaking decades later, Kennedy said he was frustrated by the "academics … telling me what we should do and 'I think this' and 'I think that'."

He said, "It just got too much for me so I just said, 'Don't think, do something!'"

This would be a better story if the sporting annals showed Hawthorn won. We lost that Saturday afternoon, but Kennedy did exact revenge the next year.

Moving from strategy to action is tough. The toughest of the tough tell us this – not just sports coaches. The *Harvard Business Review* quoted a survey of more than 400 CEOs from around the world who rated "executional excellence" as their number one challenge from some 80 management issues. This is why project management and consultancy are booming – fields dedicated to helping boards and bosses implement strategy. Wishing for action does not make it happen.

One of the workshops I run is simply titled Strategy to Action. I try to make it fun, but at the heart of it is deconstructing a plan into manageable chunks. With such a staged process we see what will happen in the short term as well as in the longer term. As an example, I might split a change program of 12 to 18 months into three stages of four to six months' duration. Each stage comprises a handful of initiatives with clearly defined outcomes. Along the continuum, you can see the smaller early wins working their way through to significant changes in the way of working.

Try this in your business. Instead of being overwhelmed by 18-month or 24-month goals, break your plan down into more manageable stages, with clearly defined goals along the way. This allows you to make adjustments if needed, and also provides motivation as you and your team celebrate milestones along the way.

The importance of good communication

Research reveals how good company-wide communication works alongside strategy implementation, a kind of lubricant that unblocks the corporate cogs. A survey by global consultants McKinsey & Co found that when managers and frontline employees were unengaged, the success rate of projects was only 3 per cent, compared with success rates of more than 25 per cent when they were involved. And the CEO's role in conveying the company strategy was critical: a transformation is 5.8 times more likely to be successful at organisations where CEOs communicate a compelling, high-level change story, and 6.3 times more likely to be successful when senior leaders share aligned messages about the change effort with the rest of the organisation.

The message: form your strategy, communicate it expertly and work actively on engagement.

That's taking action.

Your strategy team

Organisations have different approaches to how they form strategy. A collegial process is fine but someone has to be responsible for how initiatives are implemented. Big organisations have strategists to mould thinking and project management offices to execute. It can also pay to have an external facilitator come into the business. Without prejudices about people or issues, independent consultants can corral ideas and fix any communication problems. Who will lead the charge for your SMART comms plan?

CHAPTER 17

MEDIA

"The explosion in tribes, groups, covens and circles of interest means that anyone who wants to make a difference can."

MARKETER SETH GODIN, *TRIBES*

Connecting with your content communities

In newsroom-speak, "content is king". In marketing, "content is currency". They both recognise content is an asset with value.

Let me add another: content is community. In the DIY Newsroom, a chief objective is to develop a community, a tribe of followers as marketing guru Seth Godin would say.

Every business or organisation has communities of interest, which can be represented as client lists or subscribers to a newsletter. From the outset you need to be clear about why you are bothering to generate content to share with a particular community. Before you hit the record, publish, upload or post button, ask – *why?*

Ask:

- Why am I posting to our Facebook business page?
- Why am I writing blogs?

- Why am I creating video for YouTube?
- Why am I sending an email newsletter to 10,000 people?
- Why do we employ someone to post on social media every day?
- What exactly is the community of interest we are building?
- What is the point of doing all this?

The SMART Way clarifies your "why", which ultimately must relate to a tangible return on investment. Otherwise, why are you doing it? Your time and resources are finite – and, as such, your communications have to amount to more than the vanity game of chasing likes and shares.

Eight reasons why a content strategy matters

Here are eight reasons why a content strategy matters. Which resonate for you?

1. You want recognition for the great work your organisation, team and you do.
2. You want better results from your efforts and to bring prospects into your marketing funnel.
3. You want to tell people about your services, products and cause.
4. You want to craft and control your message – not let others shape your image.
5. You want to position yourself as the go-to expert in your field and become a key business of influence.
6. You want to take advantage of low- to no-cost communications.
7. You want to build a community because communities are where connections and opportunities happen.
8. You want to develop heartfelt relationships with people in your target market. You want to help them and win their business.

Understanding why you are in the content game in the first place is an essential ingredient to creating truly compelling content worth the time of a prospective audience.

Content communities at work

When I trained cadet journalists I asked them about their media consumption. What newspapers did they read? What radio and TV programs did they tune into? What magazines did they consume? I wanted them to live, eat and breathe all things media. I also wanted them to intimately understand content from an audience perspective.

What are *your* content habits? What content communities or tribes do you belong to? What piques your interest? It might be a favourite Facebook group, a magazine in the mail, or a YouTube channel.

The Qantas and AFL newsletters stand out from the crowd for me. They reflect my interests, and they are also a study in how to shape and deliver valuable information. The Qantas newsletter and its website carry engaging and visual stories about destinations I'm interested in. This content helps me make choices about restaurants, hotels and places I want to visit. AFL Media expertly uses social media to take engagement to a new level. The AFL is a tribe of tribes – 18 clubs with among the most fanatical supporter bases in the world. I receive the AFL's daily newsletter, which in the olden days would have been the sports pages of the local newspaper.

These organisations have the benefit of multi-million-dollar marketing budgets. But what really distinguishes them is they understand how to target their constituencies.

Elsewhere I refer to Australia's largest private health insurer Bupa. Through its digital newsroom, the company has successfully created a community around a mix of content, including blogs, social media posts and video – and that should be your aim. The key to success is understanding why people would want to join your community. What is in it for them?

Creating a personal brand community

What are you passionate about? A mother at our school has 15,000 followers on Instagram, gathered around her niche of '70s retro. She has leveraged this to open a shop that sells retro furniture, clothing and knick-knacks. She is the personification of creating a successful online micro-community. From there, she could produce video, a blog, a coffee table book. What would a micro-community look like built around your personal niche? What is your "thing"? Do you have a brand or certain interests? Now, think of this in terms of your organisation.

The bland, boring and banal is everywhere

Once upon a time, we did stuff – like play sport, talk directly to people and visit real shops. Today, we live our lives out on a mobile phone. Data tells us Australians spend at least two hours a day on social media.

The problem is that the more content we see the more we waste our time because most of it is rubbish. We would be far better spending our time walking the dog, taking the kids to the park or doing our hair (well, some of us).

As much as people think newspapers today are redundant, watch a paper get passed around a café. That is because it usually carries a high level of interest for a niche audience. It is written to a quality standard and to its market. Most online content that people create – from the amateur dabbler to the professional content marketer – rarely hits the mark, let alone is shared.

Rubbish content can get a life of its own as some people and businesses are very good at gaming the system, or they pay for placement.

But if that is your strategy, it's a bad one. It is highly inefficient and most likely unsustainable.

Linked in, but turned off

If you want endless examples of the bland, boring and banal, go to LinkedIn. If you want an appreciation of what *not* to do, spend time analysing its news feed – no shortage of puffed-up wannabes happy to pontificate but who have little substance, usually no style, and not a solution in sight. There is gold there somewhere, but you have to be a good miner to find it.

In a non-scientific experiment, I spent 15 minutes analysing my feed, consuming about 70 posts and reshares. Almost 75 per cent of the content was utterly irrelevant – a mix of off-target sponsored content, not-of-my-niche reshares, often with the lazy poster making no comment at all. The worst of it was the 15 per cent of content that was blatant promotion, chest-thumping or sycophancy, which had zero interest for me.

I resent this waste of time, and this is why social media platforms change their algorithms to promote more engaging and "shareable" content. The fact that quality content can be hard to find, though, presents an opportunity to those who create storytelling better than the competition.

The Eight Deadly Sins of Rubbish Content

To ensure you do not raise the ire of your audience, or fail to get one in the first place, never create content that is …

1. bland, boring and banal
2. spurious in nature (worthy of a thought bubble but not much more)
3. poorly written (get yourself the excellent, no-nonsense Strunk and White, *The Elements of Style*)
4. full of jargon and business-speak (read Don Watson's classics *Watson's Dictionary of Weasel Words* or *Death Sentence: The decay of public language*)
5. irrelevant – written for or distributed to the wrong audience
6. packaged with the wrong media (for example, video when a blog is better, or vice versa)
7. misleading, false or tricky
8. clichéd, repetitive or plagiarised.

The content revolution is coming

Please forgive my sanctimony. Most people do not deliberately create rubbish content. It is just that today anyone can be a publisher and this has lowered the bar. Thankfully, a renaissance in quality content is coming – the beautifully handcrafted, the intriguing, the unique voice.

How do I know this? Firstly, I feel it in my waters. But this feeling is supported by the mounting research that points to us getting sick of wasting our time on social media (although we still do that). We are starting to ask more of social, and of ourselves. Secondly, we are starting a movement. That's right – you and me.

Quality, of course, can be subjective. If you were to compare the same story in London's *Financial Times* and *The Sun* it is likely the former would be regarded by most as of higher "quality". The story may include the same facts, but the tone in *The Sun* would be tailored to the masses. In this case, quality relates as much to the audience as it does to the journalism.

In a business sense, quality is about providing thoughtful and helpful content and making that content experiential and immersive. You cannot do that with every piece of content, but together we can raise the bar.

Your checklists for creating great content

By having come this far you are already considering the virtues of a more targeted media approach driven by quality content. To this end, I have developed a two-pronged content credibility tool to test if your content meets the mark. It involves an interest test and a quality test.

The interest test

This is simple really. With the content interest test you are aiming for your content to be, well, *interesting*. It needs a good dose of "useful" and "newness" (in journalism that would be "newsworthiness").

Think about the next piece of content you are planning. How would it rate on the Richter scale – would it be earth shattering, or barely provide a rumble?

My 11-point interest test for great content is that it should be:

1. interesting – or, better still, compelling
2. relevant to the audience or a significant number of people
3. useful to your audience in making a decision or informing them on a subject
4. beneficial to public discourse on a subject
5. unique
6. entertaining
7. current
8. likely to be shared, "become the talk of the town", or great fodder for the internet
9. different or surprising
10. connection-worthy – intellectually or emotionally
11. about people (or animals sometimes work just as well).

If you score low on these points, keep working on your content until it punches higher. Or choose another subject. If you are really struggling, bring in some outside help.

The quality test

A communications team should be able to draw on its organisational culture and values to set expectations and standards. These will vary from business to business, but there are some givens in getting the right result. It takes planning and effort. It does not come from osmosis.

A good pasta requires fresh ingredients. Whether you used fresh or canned tomatoes, homemade or pre-packaged pasta, or high-grade or low-grade meat is evident in the eating. Quality content is the same. You can see it in the writing, editing and packaging. Quality content is free from error and trustworthy. It is targeted at the right audience. It is super relevant.

My six-point quality test for great content is that it should be:

1. superbly written and well produced – yes, that means with correct spelling, grammar, syntax and English expression
2. factual, with no known false assertions (use data and research)
3. credible
4. multi-dimensional – where possible, with more than one "voice"
5. respectful of your community's intelligence
6. packaged in a way that best conveys the "story" or message.

If this sounds a lot like the behaviours and practices of a newsroom, good.

How is your content currently measuring up against these tests?

"Try this amazing tool"

Technology has provided us with cool tools to make communicating easier. Artificial intelligence, for instance, will increasingly automate hum-drum tasks.

However, do not believe the hype when people start telling you how easy it is to produce content or proclaim that by using a particular tool you can start going out for long lunches. Yes, some tools can scrape the internet and fill your content schedule automatically. Yes, there are some applications that can make producing video easier (not "easy", though, if you want quality). But the results are vanilla at best.

I wince when I see organisations outsource their social media posting. Why let other agencies control how you are perceived?

How to generate great content ideas

Modern comms teams have high-powered skills in social media marketing and are good at disseminating information, but they often struggle with generating ideas and producing them well.

This is backed by the Sensis study I mentioned earlier that high-lighted how businesses find it difficult to produce original content.

Getting started

Sharing or repurposing others' content is one way of growing a con-tent community. Yet nothing beats producing it yourself. The secret to generating content is simple brainstorming.

I bet that over a couple of hours (and some coffee) we could gener-ate scores of story ideas for your business. This would be aside from what you would normally come across or respond to day to day. So a great starting point can simply be to make a time and sit down with a cup of Joe for a chat with your team – AKA "strategic planning".

Newsrooms are never short of ideas and never short of a story. That is their business. But processes, forums and a culture of curiosity are what surfaces these stories. You might consider a daily or weekly catch up to go through what is on your content calendar. In news-papers, we used to have lots of meetings. Too many. These meetings would include:

- a morning conference that would include a post-mortem on the previous edition and a plan for the next
- briefings of individual reporters on their assignments
- a meeting to decide website ranking and social media activity
- an afternoon conference to assign stories to pages
- a page 1 conference in the early evening
- regular section meetings and staff meetings
- off-site strategic workshops.

In the modern multi-platform newsroom, less is more. Today, many newsrooms only have a short daily stand-up meeting and then sporadic informal meetings throughout the day. But they still meet, and an open, regular forum is vital to converting ideas to living, breathing content.

The best editors also have a gut instinct for what constitutes a great story. That is not as valued as it once was because analytics are now the primary driver. Tools like Chartbeat tell us exactly what interests people and at what point they tire of a story. But the downside of analytics, like social media in general, is that they reinforce the popular, creating the echo chamber effect. While knowing your audience is vital and delivering tailored content is what we are all about, the best content often delights by surprise.

What *is* news?

When I was a newspaper editor I would be asked by community groups and members of the public how I decided what was news. It's a great question.

A 19th century American journalist famously stated that: "When a dog bites a man that is not news, but when a man bites a dog that is news". The British media baron Lord Northcliffe said: "News is what somebody, somewhere wants to suppress; all the rest is advertising". Mark Twain wrote: "news is history in its first and best form". More plain, but with a kernel of truth: "News is whatever the editor says it is".

To go for a no-nonsense definition, the *Oxford English Dictionary* says news is "information about important or interesting recent events, especially when published or broadcast" and "information not previously known".

Me? I say news is new information that evokes an emotion in us or connects us in some way to what is going on in our world.

Your vast range of media options

I am in seventh heaven when it comes to choices for storytelling today. We can tickle people's senses with an array of media methods. I would have loved that when I began as a journalist.

Here we are talking about *types* of "media" as distinct from the *platforms* on which we use that media. For example, a "presentation" is a *type* of media, which you could put together with Google Slides,

PowerPoint, Keynote or others, and your distribution channel could be Slideshare. "Video" would be the *type* of media and YouTube or Vimeo the *channel* or *platform*. (We'll look at choosing your channels later in this chapter.)

Here is a non-exhaustive list of some of your choices today for media type:

- video
- live streaming
- podcasts
- audio downloads (mp3)
- articles, blogs
- photography (picture galleries, photo essays)
- slide decks
- webinars
- presentations
- seminars, lectures
- workshops, conferences
- infographics, other graphic art
- PDF downloads
- surveys
- social media posts and content
- media releases
- messages, slogans, digital displays
- art
- music
- games
- software.

Variations of these media and new media, such as virtual reality and augmented reality, continue to pop up. We have never had more ways to communicate.

These days video is not optional

When you are deciding on which media to use, video is likely to have a central place. In fact, the choice is not whether you should use video but how you can best deploy it. Video is not everyone's natural suit, but I can guarantee you it will deliver new audiences and keep existing ones engaged.

Social media is prioritising video because the time spent looking at videos serves their commercial purposes and people enjoy the experience. Facebook's Mark Zuckerberg was unequivocal when he stated: "We see a world where video is first, with video at the heart of our apps and services".

There are lots of statistics about video that demonstrate the high ROI:

- online videos will account for more than 80 per cent of consumer internet traffic by 2020 (CISCO)
- 55 per cent of people consume videos thoroughly – the highest amount of all types of content (HubSpot, 2016)
- almost 75 per cent of B2B marketers say that video positively impacts marketing ROI (Tubular Insights, 2015).

You may want to engage professional videographers for big brand and marketing messages, but you can go DIY for the bulk of your video. Really? Absolutely. It is more straightforward to produce than you may think – and incredibly fun and infectious.

For the most part, keep it short and sweet. Videos up to two minutes receive the highest engagement, and viewership then drops off. The killer combination is video and mobile. More than 50 per cent of videos are watched on mobiles, according to video platform Ooyala, and that figure is rising.

Video has a bunch of applications. You can use it to repurpose blogs, for "how tos", or to provide short, snappy professional tips in your area of expertise. You do not need a heap of gear and you can quickly and effectively develop a video personality. And if you do not have skills, send someone to a short course and watch the results soar.

Your template for a content plan

Does your communications team have a content plan? Many have a marketing plan approved by management or the board, yet when it comes to the day-to-day activity of the comms team it is often assumed everything is under control. A good content plan is essential for a DIY Newsroom to run an effective operation, and in tumultuous waters it provides ballast.

Your content plan will have numerous inputs, some of which we have already considered, such as audience identification, and others I detail in subsequent chapters. Here is a simple template to create a useful content plan. List these sub-headings and flesh out as required:

- **Organisational goals**: What is the chief objective of your organisation? This could be your mission or strategic initiatives. What are you in the business of doing?
- **Communications goals:** What are the key initiatives of your comms team (now your DIY Newsroom) that will support your business objectives? Why are you "doing content"?
- **Communications approach:** How will you go about achieving your objectives? For example, the goal might be to build a community of content around four specific topic areas, and "we will do this by targeting [these audiences] through [this media] and across [these channels]".
- **Goals:** These are the specific metrics you will track to gauge the return on investment from your DIY Newsroom … and why your CEO will fall in love with the comms teams as your dashboard shows upticks and the business enjoys the knock-on effects.

- **Inputs:** This could be hyperlinks to work you have already done, such as:
  - health check
  - audience ID
  - content audit
  - content schedule/calendar.
- **Whatever else you feel is appropriate:** For example, you could attach the specific newsroom initiatives you plan to undertake for the next quarter, half-year and year.

The pièce de résistance of your content plan, though, is a simple visual of your network of communication channels – your media ecosystem.

Choosing your weapons of mass communication

"Know the enemy and know yourself."

SUN TZU (545–470 BC), CHINESE GENERAL AND REPUTED
AUTHOR OF *THE ART OF WAR*

At the heart of a good DIY Newsroom is your media ecosystem. Without a documented network, without thinking about and settling on how you plan to create, package and distribute your communications, you will be a lost soul in the vast wilderness of the web.

You would be amazed at the number of organisations, from small non-government organisations through to big corporates, that do not give this enough thought.

In forming a content ecosystem you will consider, evaluate and carefully select the communication channels you will use. This is where we bring method to the madness of information today. In designing your content ecosystem, you will distil your thinking to a single sheet of paper or slide – a chart that shows the constellation of channels you use or will use and what you use each one for.

These channels are your weapons of mass communication. They will distribute your messages with precision and power. A military metaphor is apt because you are involved in a battle for hearts and minds. Consider that you will be going into battle in:

- **dense, dark jungles** where your message has to cut through billions of pieces of information to see the light of day
- **mountains and ravines** where you are exposed to guerrilla-like sniping from the enemy
- **the skies** where it is fast, high-octane and not for the faint of heart
- **the flats** where traditional combat is played out.

So let's see how you should go about choosing your media channels.

Weapons of choice

Your media ecosystem must reflect your circumstances and capabilities. This requires customisation, and as time moves along new platforms may emerge that suit you better than what you once relied upon. That said, it would be remiss of me not to give you a basic guide to the pros and cons of the main channels as they stand at the time of writing and how they might fit in a DIY Newsroom.

CHOOSING YOUR MEDIA CHANNELS

Channel	Good for ...	Things to consider ...
Website	Repository and distribution point for core content, including: • product description, about you and your company • blogs, video, media room • sign-ups to other content. **You have control.**	• Most web traffic comes via search or social and not direct. • You need a complementary digital strategy. • SEO/SEM of benefit.
Email newsletter	Among the most effective marketing tools: • great way to ignite, build and leverage a content community • inexpensive • can target segments with niche content • analytics to understand each customer. **You have control.**	• Like any online tool, as more people use it, it's harder to get cut through. • You will get unsubscribes if you fail to maintain relevance and quality. • Consistency in content and timing is crucial. • Creating content takes skill, energy and time.
Traditional media (e.g. printed newsletters, brochures)	The power of print is real: • it shows authority • it provides the "real feel". **You have control.**	• Print can be expensive and time consuming to produce. • It's seen as "old school". • Distribution is harder than social media.

Channel	Good for ...	Things to consider ...
Landing pages	Independent web pages are increasingly used for individual campaigns or activities because they: • provide focus on a specific product or initiative • are attention grabbing. **You have control.**	• SEO/SEM help may be required. • Trial and error will be required to see what works.
Social media: general	What more can we say? In a nutshell: • It's accessible and arguably democratic as anyone can publish. • It's cheap and instantaneous. • You have a global audience. **BUT you DO NOT have control.**	• ROI can be hard to establish. • It can be a time waster. • Engagement requires vigilance. • It can be risky. • Data, analytics and information can be hard to verify. • It's blocked in some countries. • Platforms have quirks. • Organic reach is dwindling. Now it is user pays.
Facebook	World's biggest content platform. You have to be there: • Ideal for engagement and "the conversation". • Pages give your business a home, groups spur animated conversation, Messenger connects, FB ads are cheap and generally good at targeting customers.	• Continued concerns about privacy and use of data. • Ads and boosting can rope in audience you do not want. • Hard to be heard if you do not pay to boost. • Have to work at it. • Unpredictable because of algorithm changes. • Currently blocked in China.

Channel	Good for ...	Things to consider ...
Facebook (cont.)	• A primary channel for distributing or promoting announcements, blogs, photos and other content. • Gives video a wide and deep audience. • FB Live – use it. • Excellent analytics. • Regular new features.	• For maximum impact you have to post "natively". **It controls you.**
Twitter	With 280-character tweets, is the modern news wire (think Associated Press, Reuters): • Home of intelligentsia – people in media, politics, peak organisations. • Good for linking to other content. • Can respond quickly to situations.	• Anything commercial (unless paid for) gets shot down. • Good stuff can get lost amid amateurs, time-wasters. • Choose words wisely. Context not possible in 280 characters. • Wobbly business model. **You do not control.**
YouTube	Google-owned home of how-to video: • Potential reach huge. • Establish your own channels. • Place to go viral.	• Producing video can be time-consuming. Make it simple. • Sheer volume of video. **You do not control.**
Instagram	Visual star of the social media show, Instagram is owned by Facebook: • Showcase your people and culture, and build brand. • Relatively high engagement per visit. • Place to reach younger demographic.	• Cannot link from posts. • Needs consistency and commitment. **You do not control.**

Channel	Good for ...	Things to consider ...
in LinkedIn	Social's home of business banter: • With paid-for add-ons, powerful way to target and communicate with business leaders. • Highlight thought leadership. • Virtual connection can lead to real connections. • Not blocked in China.	• Tosh central. Home of sycophancy, high-fiving, inspiring but shallow storytelling. • Your gold can get lost in the mish-mash. • Algorithm changes. • Moving to user pays model. • May need to bring in expertise. **It controls you.**
Snapchat	More popular now than Twitter, Snapchat is a recreational photo/video sharing platform for young people: • Reaches younger demographic. • Creative storytelling. • Home of A-list celebrities.	• Many companies have struggled to incorporate (with notable exceptions). • Will the business model survive? • Unverified and questionable content. **It controls you.**
Pinterest	"Helps you find ideas to try" – a social media pinboard: • Niche communities love it (crafts, cooking, etc.). • Female audience.	• Does it do anything the other social players do not? • Relatively small following.
WeChat, RenRen, Weibo	Millions of people use apps and services that many in the Western World would not know exist. In China, a staggering number of people, as well as ex-pats, use WeChat: • Reach foreign-based markets.	• Need expertise (foreign language) and an international marketing plan. • In China, social channels are tightly controlled.

Channel	Good for ...	Things to consider ...
Messaging apps	Variety of new channels to engage customers and audiences: • Ease of use. • Instant and embedded in daily online/mobile experience. • Great for announcements and notifications.	• Fleeting messaging. • Must be targeted or messaging can build resentment. • Spam.
Podcasts	Podcasting has become a niche media industry with various platforms gaining popularity: • Brilliant for storytelling, showcasing thought leadership. • Low to no cost.	• Time consuming to produce and sustain. • Requires excellent interviewing skills. • Technical setup. • Getting talent. • Building an audience takes time.

The many factors in deciding your channels

This is what does a lot of marketers' and business leaders' heads in. Which channels to distribute what information on? How many channels to use? What are the ones to prioritise? Having a thorough understanding of the merits and pitfalls of each platform will make the decision far easier.

You should ask yourself a series of questions to help you decide which channels to use. Here is a checklist you can implement as part of the SMART process:

• How many channels, traditional and new media, can you realistically sustain?

• What does each platform involve?

• Who will look after each channel? Do you have the in-house skills? Do you require additional support or training?

- How does each channel align with your communication goals?
- Of your content, what is best suited for each channel?
- Where do your audiences congregate – and what for? Which channels give you the most direct route to those audiences?
- Which channels suit the tone and personality of your organisation?
- How can you reach influencers who will endorse or promote your brand?
- How will you gauge success?

Seeking input from your people

The centrepiece for the communication reviews I do for companies is a right-sized, customised ecosystem, with an accompanying explanation of how each channel is to be used. Given the importance of this, you want to make fact-based decisions. Your information gathering to help with this could include:

- surveying your audiences about what information they want and how they want it packaged
- staging focus groups
- holding "town halls" within your organisation to brief staff and to gain feedback
- evaluating social media data and patterns.

If you are considering dramatic change, collaborate with affected parties at the earliest point possible. It is basic change management: every stage you delay bringing people into the tent, buy-in is further compromised.

As well, do not discount the gut instinct of your experienced people along with others with corporate knowledge. You may want a consultant to facilitate the process.

When you feel you have the information needed, convene a workshop to decide your strategic direction. This will include determining your central channels, the traditional ones you will use, and your primary and secondary social channels.

Channel control: who has the remote?

A first principle of establishing your ecosystem is that you must be the master of your destiny. That means controlling your main channels and not leaving your content to the vagaries of social media.

At a simplistic level, the hub for your content is likely to be your website. Social media needs to be put in place as an effective yet complementary force. If your business leans too heavily on any particular social channel, this is a dangerous strategy. For one, social media is avaricious. It needs to be constantly fed, and often you do not get a commensurate return. Conversely, if you do not put anything into the relationship your social media return will wither.

This has caught a lot of people out, sometimes because of poor advice from marketing "experts" and sometimes from over-exuberance spurred by initial social media success.

You might post, upload, tweet, blog and distribute all manner of content across YouTube, Instagram, LinkedIn, Twitter, Snapchat and so on to great success, but understand you have no more control over those platforms than the alignment of the planets. You are handing over your content for free to those companies to monetise.

You *do* have control over your website. You *do* control the content and distribution of your electronic direct mail (EDMs, AKA email newsletters). If you publish hard-copy newsletters, newspapers or magazines, you *do* control them. Similarly, if you have a radio frequency, TV channel, podcast, webinar or video show that runs on your website, you hold the remote control.

But, hang on, plenty of small businesses have shot to stardom because of social media. There are hundreds, well, thousands – tens of thousands? – of cases of individuals and organisations that have created an audience around niche content on YouTube. And on regular Facebook Live sessions. Is that not one of the benefits of going DIY?

Yes. Just go in with your eyes wide open. Because what Facebook, YouTube and those titans of tech giveth, they can also taketh away with one piece of code. Let's consider the variables.

Algorithms

Social media companies regularly change their algorithms, which determine how content is ranked. In three years, Facebook changed its algorithms more than 20 times. Such changes can have a massive impact on your traffic and other results if you have a socially led (controlled) business. Changes in early 2018 saw a marked decline in traffic across Facebook for businesses, brands and media.

Facebook and other platforms such as LinkedIn are trying to reconcile keeping us hugely engaged (more and more from us interacting, commenting and posting – not just reading) while sustaining a commercial model for themselves. We should not be surprised when our individual goals do not align with those of global enterprises.

Scrutiny and regulation

The growth of social media has outpaced and outwitted governments and regulators, but the authorities are now getting in the game.

There has been a growing backlash against Facebook. Also, traditional media is turning up the heat, leading many of us to question the use of our data to guide political and other interests. Let's not forget, Facebook has the biggest collection of personal data ever. Even big consumers of social media do not trust social media, research shows.

Any added scrutiny introduces uncertainty for those doing business on the platform. In the least, it brings into question the integrity of and trust in those platforms.

Economics

Tech companies have driven most of the growth in recent years in the booming US stock market. The sector underpins millions of jobs. Reaping US$40 billion in ad sales in 2017, Facebook is big business. It is also vulnerable, like all companies, to financial, political and social factors.

In the wake of the Cambridge Analytica data scandal in March 2018, Facebook's share price fell 8.5 per cent, wiping US$45 billion off its market value. Twitter, as we know, has experienced its own instability. Will it be there in another five years?

These platforms have been a cheap way to promote your services – but when these businesses tighten up their operations, the cost of social marketing will increase. And some platforms will crash and burn. Do not go down with them.

Whims and fashions

Clever organisations have created appealing content that goes viral, providing extraordinary impact. My Kiwi friend and comms maestro David King and his team at Ryman Healthcare did this with a brilliant video of seniors miming Pharrell Williams's song *Happy*. The video has many millions of views on YouTube. The video is effective because of the fresh angle and "wow" factor.

Many organisations and individuals spend a lot of energy trying to fabricate such social media sugar hits, which is exhausting and usually unsuccessful because you can't simply "make something go viral". Such businesses operate in a world where likes and shares have become a dopamine-driven drug of dependence, which leaves them subject to the whims of social media users, not the masters of a strategic social media plan.

The business models of Instagram, LinkedIn and Snapchat, in particular, rely on the power of influencers to gather a crowd. Nothing could go wrong there, huh? *The Wall Street Journal* reported pop star

Rihanna erased US$800 million from Snapchat's market value in March 2018 with one post when she took exception to a joke that trivialised the assault on her by her ex-boyfriend. The month prior, Snapchat shares dropped more than 6 per cent (US$1.3 billion) when Kylie Jenner posted she did not use the app anymore.

The same principles of SMART apply whether you are a corporate organisation or an A-list celebrity – you maximise your outcomes if you are strategic, use the right media (controlling it, not letting it control you) and you produce original, relevant and engaging content authentically aligned with your brand.

Social media platforms are hugely subject to whims and fashions. Never forget that.

* * *

Digital and social media puts the DIY in the DIY Newsroom. However, social media brings with it a bunch of uncertainty that we need to acknowledge in our hierarchy of channels.

Joe Pulizzi, the founder and CEO of the Content Marketing Institute, says we should build content assets where we have the maximum amount of control. Fans, followers and subscribers are not of equal value, he writes in *Content Inc.* Rather, he rates email subscribers at the top of the tree, followed by print subscribers, LinkedIn connections, Twitter subscribers, iTunes and others, with Facebook fans at the bottom. This might all change, but you get the principle.

Says Pulizzi: "You should leverage Facebook however you can, but you need to know that Facebook controls the ultimate reach, not you".

Tara Hunt, a social media expert, provides an apt metaphor: we would not build a mansion on rented land controlled by an unpredictable landholder. Why then would we surrender control of our content to platforms owned by others for them to monetise?

Developing your hierarchy of channels

Okay, let's establish your hierarchy of channels. There is no right or wrong, but I am suggesting this as a playbook.

Central channel

It's a contradiction in terms to maintain more than one central channel, so let me nominate that for most organisations it will be their website.

In itself, a business website will not drive content, but it should be the hub of everything you do. What you will find is that if your ecosystem is set up right – and is simple enough – your other channels will drive web traffic for you through search and social or via direct links.

Your central content hub does not *have* to be a website. Electronic direct mail (EDM or email newsletters) is an excellent way to build an audience and can be your main tool. But most EDMs draw on content from where? Your website.

In the case of traditional media, the central platform is all important and is what distinguishes each organisation and their audience. It could be an app, newspaper, website, radio station, TV station and so forth. They might use various channels, but there is always a central one on which their business model is founded. For example, a television station might also have a website, podcast and Facebook page, but TV is still the central channel.

Rarely would I see a social media platform as being a central channel.

Traditional channels

Traditional channels, those delivery mechanisms familiar to anyone over the age of 40, get a bad rap amid the digital zeal. Some modern media agencies look down their noses at anything to do with print, such as magazines, hard-copy newsletters and brochures, journals, reports and, heaven forbid, books. But you have more control over these channels than social media, and so they should be included in your hierarchy.

Some activities on your calendar will be best covered by traditional media. For example, in the education sector, this could be internal and external announcements, in-person staff meetings and assemblies. School yearbooks are treasured keepsakes. Who wants a "soft version"?

But, some traditional means are worth rethinking if there are more effective digital options. Apply your SMARTs.

Social channels

A main function of social channels is to redistribute or repurpose content from your website. This is where we can get excited – and get it wrong.

I split social channels into primary and secondary. Primary is where your focus should be. Let's take a look.

Primary social channels

Facebook pages and, increasingly, Facebook groups fall into the primary social channel category for many organisations. LinkedIn can also help individuals, brands and organisations build their profile and to distribute content to niche audiences.

Social media has spawned an industry of experts who will show you how to build your business around individual platforms. Make sure this aligns with your wider business strategy. You do not want to regurgitate and repeat your content across every social platform. Posts needs to be tailored to each platform. I use Buffer, but you may find something else more suitable.

While much of your content will reside in original format on your website, you will create communications specifically for social – from tweets through to video.

Think, for example, about what will be your home for video. It makes sense to embed video on your website and on landing pages, but to also share video to your YouTube channel. YouTube, in this case, would be a primary channel. You could link from other social channels back to your website or to YouTube. Or you could post the video natively into LinkedIn or Facebook, which those platforms favour above links.

There is no correct answer. But avoid overthinking this and creating a spaghetti junction as you map every-which-way-possible your content can be distributed.

Start with a strategy, experiment and confirm "your way".

Secondary social channels

Secondary does not mean token. You do not set up social accounts without a purpose, to lay dormant. Everyone you know might have a Snapchat account, but it should not have a place in your ecosystem unless there is a reason. Think of a secondary channel as that hybrid club in your golf bag for those special moments on the course. Or as a secondary line of attack that mops up the stragglers.

Use secondary channels:

- to reach a niche or unfamiliar audience
- for impact, because an audience is unaccustomed to seeing you in that space
- for a particular moment or event
- to advertise.

Social marketing – paid ads, boosts and other promotions – is likely to have a place in your operations. The days of a free kick in front of goal from social media are over. You can save yourself a lot of time and uncertainty by paying to target users rather than hoping for organic reach. Paid social marketing can also bring valuable traffic to a video, blog or campaign – and you should consider this as you frame your marketing budget.

* * *

How you describe your ecosystem is less important than what you do operationally. What matters is that you select the best weapons for the conditions (they do not have to be the most powerful) and that you can sustain their use. No point being in the open field and running out of ammo (resources). Periodically review your ROI and promote or relegate channels accordingly.

A critical consideration in forming your ecosystem is where you want traffic to go and what for. Some businesses and marketing teams value traffic for traffic's sake, but what most business really want is engagement that leads to sales conversions or achieves strategic objectives.

An ecosystem fit for the times

The following image shows the net result of this process: a visual of your constellation of channels. The aim is to put light years between you and the competition. Once you have this ecosystem, you have the blueprint for a DIY Newsroom.

You can add more information to it if you like. You could expand on the ecosystem further by:

- adding targets for each channel or key activities
- documenting overall objectives (a good reminder)
- marrying the ecosystem with the content schedule (see "How to create a content calendar" later in this chapter) or other SMART outputs
- describing the media you will use for each channel.

CONSTELLATION OF CHANNELS

Here's my ecosystem of media channels. It continues to evolve – just like the rest of the universe. Behind each channel is a distinct but not elaborate strategy. Social media is a complementary force. For the most part, individual platforms favourably rank content that is posted natively.

Website
Mothership. While it is not the main touchpoint for audiences, it acts as a repository and distribution hub for content

Email
Newsletters with premium content that is honed for target audiences

Print
Premium content distributed via publications, brochures, this book!

Secondary channels
Use of other organisation's channels – e.g. external media and networks run by industry associations

Primary social media
Tailored and repurposed content posted directly to Facebook, YouTube

Secondary social media
Channels used as required, but consistently enough to maintain a presence and following – Twitter, LinkedIn, Instagram, Slideshare

Staying up to date

Who do you have on reconnaissance? You need someone with a constant eye on the media landscape – and to look over the horizon. There are stacks of blogs and resources to help you gather intel. Combined with your own analytics and thinking, you can take advantage of new technologies or movements and stay ahead of the competition.

Why print still matters

"In 10 to 15 years, people will look at a newspaper and laugh."

CHICAGO MEDIA EXECUTIVE TALKING TO THE AUTHOR IN 1996

The power of print was evident to me in the first week of my job as a cadet journalist at a small country newspaper. One of my duties – as well as writing – was to deliver the paper to newsagents, hot off the press.

The editor lit up another ciggie and kept the motor running while I delivered bundles of papers, outlet by outlet. This was in 1984, and people milled around the counter to get their hands on their weekly digest of local news, to check if their kids' sports results were published, and to catch up on the town chit-chat. It was tremendous validation as a journalist that the work I did had value.

In the past decade or so, newspapers have been under siege. Across the globe, newspaper advertising revenue and circulation have plummeted dramatically. Australia and Oceania (including New Zealand) has experienced among the steepest declines, a loss of towards 25 per cent over five years, according to the WAN-IFRA World Press Trends survey.

But I believe there is life left in the old girl yet. Over more than 30 years working in the industry I have seen all the ups and downs of newspapers. I continue to work with companies with significant print holdings, and my mission is helping them to save their newspapers – or at least make them stronger for longer.

This is not just because I am romantic about newspapering, but because print does things digital cannot.

More than ink on dead trees

Here are five reasons why print still matters:

1. **Print = trust:** Research shows even the millennials, who have no affinity with traditional media, trust print more than other

sources, particularly social media. The Yellow Social Media Report 2018 found 73 per cent of those surveyed trusted traditional news sources, including print media, well above what appeared from news sources on social media (16 per cent) or from friends and family posts on social media on what was happening (11 per cent). As well, a third of respondents admitted to reacting to something on social media that they later discovered was untrue. Digital gets our attention, but print gets our respect.

2. **Print is tactile:** The tangibility of print ignites senses in a different way to what we see on a screen. A marketing colleague of mine tells the story of how she was pitching an idea to a prospect. It was hard going, until she presented him with a brochure that succinctly described the package on offer. Sold. Print provides us with a comforting lay-back experience. Nothing better than a macchiato and the morning newspaper.

3. **Print is utilitarian:** Newspapers, magazines and brochures have proven to be enduring formats. The mobile phone is the ultimate utilitarian device, but you can do a lot with paper too. The best print products curate what we need to know and enlighten us about the world without us having to trawl across the world wide web and mentally piecing it together.

4. **Print is permanent:** We process, retain and recall information better via print. A Temple University (US) study found paper beat digital in a host of areas, including for creating an emotional reaction and a desire for a product or service. The study found print marketing activated the ventral striatum of the brain more than digital media. Another study found physical material was more real to the brain and hence could be categorised and processed. Print has impact and permanency.

5. **Print is swag:** Print is the new digital. It has fresh currency in a digital world where everyone has a website and lives out their personal and business existences ostentatiously on social media. *The Economist* honours the written word in its beautiful

formulaic weekly news magazine. *Monocle* is a monthly magazine that exudes a strong internationalist, hip personality. A HarperCollins executive told my New York study tour in 2017 that Amazon's online sales of print titles had soared 15 per cent year on year. Why the resurgence? Printed books hold people's attention and are permanent. And 18- to 29-year-olds were most likely to read books. Print is still beautiful.

I'm sure it is not lost on you that, for all these reasons and more, I committed to putting my best thinking down on paper. In print. In a book.

How can print fit into your ecosystem?

Whether you are a business, council, educational institution, non-profit or elite sporting body, bespoke printed products can connect you to your target market. With print, you can put yourself, your organisation, in the hands of existing customers and prospects.

You can use print in a targeted and creative way for rebranding, campaign launches and histories and anniversaries. Print is a magnificent third-party tool. Provide books (like this one!) to your clients as a value add. Tell your stories in a photographic compendium – in print.

In print, consider:

- regular direct mail newsletters, newspapers and magazines
- high-quality brochures, flyers and booklets
- yearbooks or annual reports
- artistically designed infographics, wall charts, and posters
- artwork
- informative books or coffee-table books
- calendars.

How to create a content calendar

*"Plan your work for today and every day,
then work your plan."*

FORMER BRITISH PRIME MINISTER MARGARET THATCHER

A content calendar is the culmination of your planning – a reference guide to what you post, how you post, where you post to, and when. Just going through the process of creating a calendar is a worthwhile exercise in thinking through the SMART steps and aligning content to your wider objectives.

The five key steps are:

1. Get your ducks in a row.
2. Select your tools.
3. Create a monthly content calendar template.
4. Add the content.
5. Meet, schedule, meet, schedule.

Let's have a look at each of these.

Get your ducks in a row

Don't even think about creating a calendar template until you have:

- mapped your content – conduct an audit of what you do now and what content you can access, and analyse the gaps
- identified your audiences
- chosen your network of channels.

These are addressed in chapters 16 and 17.

Select your tools

What should you use for creating your content template? I use Google apps for most of my business because of its online prowess and the ability to collaborate. Any decent-sized operation will benefit from the more popular social media management tools. Or sometimes you cannot beat simplicity, online connectivity and a good ol' fashioned spreadsheet.

There are many options available, so do your homework and create a system that meets your needs. Having good systems in place for the creation and distribution of your content plan will save you a truckload of time.

Create a monthly content calendar template

Now create a generic monthly calendar of content that is realistically within your capacity to deliver. A starting point is to slot in the number of posts you are thinking of for each channel across each week. You can then be more specific; for instance, specify that you will run a blog on your website on Wednesday and then post it to LinkedIn on Thursday and share it on Facebook a week later.

Add the content

What will you post over the next month? With a basic structure in place, you can now break it down and specify the content for each item. Make a copy of your template for each month and insert your intended content for the coming month.

Meet, schedule, meet, schedule

Start this process with a team meeting, and once it's up and running you should meet and review your schedule at least weekly. Make sure you take into account what worked and what didn't work from the previous month, and adjust your plans accordingly.

The golden rule

Yes, treat everyone as you would have them treat you. Regarding content, treat every piece of content as an opportunity to use in different ways. Put simply, repurpose every piece of content you can.

Let's say you run a sports academy. The academy dietician has provided you with a terrific three-day, pre-game, carb-loaded menu. What could you do with that? It could start as a blog on your website – a short introduction and the recipes for each meal. From there you could repurpose it as:

- YouTube videos
- subject matter for your e-newsletter
- contributions to the local newspaper, specialist sport and food magazines
- Facebook and Instagram posts
- a podcast interview with the sports dietician who provided the content.

Start with a master story and deconstruct it using text, vision, audio and images for dissemination across channels. Go forth and multiply! You'll get much more leverage from your content by repurposing it for different audiences and different channels.

CHAPTER 18

AUTHENTICITY

"Eighty-one per cent of Facebook users had little to no confidence in Facebook to protect their data and privacy."

BUSINESS INSIDER INTELLIGENCE 2018 DIGITAL TRUST SURVEY

Why authenticity matters today more than ever

As a journalist and truth seeker, I am not a fan when terms are bandied around casually and without basis. An example is when you hear politicians talk about the "unique Australian value of mateship". What, that's not common elsewhere? It is hardly unique.

Similarly, we hear a lot about trust never being as valuable as it is today. And how we are searching for authenticity. In this case, it is more than a cliché. Trust is the new currency in business, and there is lots of evidence to explain why it has escalated in the global conversation.

A good part of that is because of disruption: we have undergone unprecedented technological change in recent years. This will continue to occur – more change, and at a faster rate. As a consequence, society and the way we live our lives have been rocked. We are doing many things we never did before.

In such times of tumult, we look for those things that ground us, give us comfort and reflect our core as humans. Therein lies our search for those in whom we can trust.

Institutional breakdown

In sector after sector, organisations and individuals have been exposed for who they really are, and it doesn't match the slick marketing or PR that have given them a veneer of respectability.

Churches have lost their moral authority because their leaders have perpetrated or covered up the evils that they preach against. Our banks have profited by billions of dollars while ripping properties from drought-affected farmers who never missed a mortgage payment. In sport, some of the nation's and the world's most esteemed competitors have been caught cheating. In politics, we continue to see the bar on standards lowered.

Technology? It was meant to propel us to new heights and new opportunities, but it too has turned on us. We are more educated, more connected and richer than ever. But what has happened to societal values? The great democratisation of media – the ability for anyone to publish – has created a jungle of communications. Facebook has allowed strangers to invade our privacy, steal our data and cook elections. The Russians have brought us fake news (that is, *actual* fake news stories, not the Trump version of "fake news", which is just anything that criticises him), and every day we learn of another data breach and threat to our security.

Mad as hell

This has all created growing global cynicism and distrust. Tellingly, the 2018 Edelman Trust Barometer shows that 20 of the 28 countries that it surveyed are "distrusters".

I am reminded of that terrific scene in *Network* where Peter Finch's character, newscaster Howard Beale, reaches the end of his tether and rages on TV against the system:

> *I want you to get MAD! I don't want you to protest. I don't want you to riot – I don't want you to write to your congressman, because I wouldn't know what to tell you to write. I don't know what to do about the depression and the inflation and the Russians and the crime in the street. All I know is that first you've got to get mad. You've got to say: "I'm a human being, god-dammit! My life has value! ... go to the window. Open it, and stick your head out and yell: I'M AS MAD AS HELL, AND I'M NOT GOING TO TAKE THIS ANYMORE.*

That was written some 40 years, but it still resonates. It is the sentiment that gave us Donald Trump.

The rise of Trump

In politics, when people have had enough of the incumbents, they turn off or they get mad as hell and rise up. In the US, they did the latter and elected Donald Trump. Trump tapped into a disenchanted and disenfranchised middle America. Globalism was not working for them. This was perfect fodder for the Trump camp, which spoke to them, spoke for them, and grew into a political juggernaut and then a movement.

Forbes magazine wrongly stated in a piece published in July 2015 that "despite all of the hoopla ... the Donald will never sit in the Oval Office". But it nailed the simmering sentiment behind the Trump phenomena:

> *As bizarre as it might be, could he actually be the only catalytic agent capable of initiating a paradigm shift in politics? ... Donald just may be the political anomaly, outlier and black swan all wrapped up in one that can finally illuminate for Americans the*

*highly dysfunctional, polarized political system that is simply
collapsing, like a black hole, under its own weight. Having reduced
politics over the past decades to sound bites, trigger-finger polls,
ideological litmus tests, handlers, endless fundraising, cronyism and
politics-as-entertainment are we simply getting what we deserve?
Donald Trump is the logical conclusion to the breakdown of the
American political system.*

Trump, disruption, our search for trust – it is a new world, and a
new opportunity for SMART communicators.

The reputation sweet spot

"Always do right. This will gratify some people and astonish the rest."

AMERICAN WRITER MARK TWAIN (1835–1910)

The Edelman Trust research provides remarkable validation of the value of building authentic relationships with your audience. If you mean what you say and do what you say, people will believe you, follow you and do business with you.

The Edelman data shows:

- company content is twice as trusted by customers when there is an existing relationship, which is at the core of what we are developing in the DIY Newsroom
- content produced in such a context is more trusted than content produced by journalists
- a company's social media is more believable than its advertising (63 per cent versus 37 per cent).

On the whole, the survey implores businesses and their leaders to get in the game. The public believes good business is socially led business that puts as much energy into the community conversation as it does into generating economic prosperity.

Some 56 per cent of respondents agreed that companies that only thought about themselves and their profits were bound to fail. And four in five respondents believed CEOs had an obligation to speak out on issues such as the economy, automation, global warming, discrimination and education. But most of what we hear today is corporate messaging and glorified brand promotion. We want more valuable insights. The public wants to hear opinions, arguments and contributions that will lead to better policy, outcomes, and quality of life for all of us.

This is the social purpose sweet spot. Those organisations that can create authentic and creative content while also making a contribution to society will stand out. It's a radical departure from the conventions of old-school public relations and corporate comms, which was all about the saying, not the doing.

What do we mean by "acting credibly"?

Aussie Rules is a big corporate by any standard. The AFL draws huge crowds, mammoth broadcast deals, and regularly features on both the back and front pages of the newspapers. For me, it also epitomises the principles and practices of a successful DIY Newsroom. This is not surprising, given it was set up by a former senior journalist who knows all about newsrooms.

AFL Media head of content Matthew Pinkney says trust and authenticity have powered the game's communications success in recent years. A former reporter with Melbourne's footy-obsessed tabloid newspaper, the *Herald Sun*, he brought a hard-nosed approach to an extremely commercially sensitive environment when he began building the AFL's newsroom in 2012. Said Pinkney:

> *My approach has always been that unless we are authentic and unless we are prepared to tell difficult stories about the AFL and its clubs and its players we won't retain an audience. So as soon as people think we are basically creating a marketing outlet or a Pravda-style spin shop we'll lose that audience and we'll lose the benefits that flow.*

This telling of the truth is not as easy as it sounds. Administrators and CEOs are usually quite comfortable with the concept – until they have to tell news that may not reflect favourably on them and their businesses. Pinkney again:

> *It's simple to say [be authentic] but it is hard to implement. I have asked a few retailers who were looking at setting up similar operations to the AFL, if they would be prepared to do a list of the best five nappies in Australia on price versus something and have*

themselves at number two. They said of course not. Well, unless you're prepared to do things like that you're not going to maintain a loyal audience who believes in you.

Audiences now are hyper informed … You can't just say this is what it is – people will go and find their own truth. If you are telling the truth in the first instance and they've gone off and found that is the truth then they'll trust you. But otherwise they're not going to trust you.

Some social media safeguards

Unfortunately, there is bound to come a time when your reputation is threatened by the actions of trolls or the misadventure of your staff. But there are two preventative measures you can put into place: a social media account register and a social media policy.

- **Social media account register**

  This is a database that lists your social media accounts and the names and details of those with administration, manager and user access. Whoever is running the comms team should keep a secure record of user names and passwords (not on a spreadsheet that everyone can see). You may be unpleasantly surprised by what accounts you have in your organisation.

  I also recommend keeping a record of any "unofficial" accounts. I've had clients who have found well-intentioned parties have set up accounts that give the impression they have an official endorsement. One client was staggered to identify 20 "unofficial" accounts. Most were okay, but the exercise headed off at least one catastrophe.

- **Social media policy**

  Do your staff understand your expectations about their use of social media accounts in your name, and where personal and professional use can overlap? Be clear and emphatic with staff about what they can and cannot do in their official capacity and what they post about the business when not on your time.

The social dividends of being authentic

"Truth is its own reward."

GREEK PHILOSOPHER PLATO

Authentic communication is a noble and righteous endeavour. But being authentic has to be more than a company catch phrase. There needs to be a real connection between how an organisation speaks about its endeavours and what it does in practice. How do you feel, for instance, when you see a stunningly shot commercial with a moving story, only to find the ad is flogging insurance? It jars.

Be it corporate social responsibility or social purpose, connecting brands with deeper meaning has become a busy marketplace. As such, there is a widening gulf between those companies that are making a heartfelt connection with audiences and those that are essentially engaged in a cynical marketing exercise.

In the former category is the social enterprise created by one of my clients in New Zealand, Stuff. The company has set up a coffee shop at its Auckland offices staffed by deaf baristas. Hundreds of employees have learned basic sign language to order their daily cup of Joe. The Coffee Co-op is a showcase of what people with disabilities can do instead of focusing on what they cannot. From a communications perspective, the enterprise has provided management and staff with an inspiring human interest story to share about diversity and inclusion.

Delivering genuine and authentic initiatives and communications can provide similar benefits for your organisation. There are five clear social dividends:

1. **Doing good is good for business:** Open and transparent communications makes you more trustworthy, and people will more likely want to do business with you. According to Colmar Brunton, which runs New Zealand's reputation index,

the higher your credibility the more likely your products and services will be purchased or recommended. Sunday Lunch, a Sydney-based consultancy that helps brands leverage social good, cites research that 80 per cent of people would be willing to buy from unknown brands if they had strong social and environmental credentials.

2. **Reputation inoculation:** Despite getting a flu shot, you can still catch the flu – but it's much less likely and the impact will not be as severe. The same goes for building your brand reputation. One of my clients suffered a terrible scandal, but it handled the ensuing communications superbly. The feedback was strongly positive because of the organisation's no-nonsense and transparent approach. Samsung's exploding Galaxy Note 7 episode and VW's emissions controversy cost both of those companies billions of dollars. But according to *Forbes*, it would have been far worse had they not accrued goodwill with consumers in years prior.

3. **Style AND substance:** I abhor the shallowness of a lot of social media, but when done well social media can crank up the vibe for your brand. If your communications can reflect a deeper connection for people as well, there is the quinella: messaging that grabs attention and resonates in the longer term.

4. **Make people feel great again:** Inherently, most of us want to make a positive difference. Acting authentically means connecting what we do in the day-to-day with a deeper purpose. Communicating the positives and making people feel good about themselves and your brand is the antidote to the cynicism that surrounds us. What would you rather be known as: a spin doctor or an inspiring storyteller?

5. **You control your message:** It's a simple equation. The more you are respected, the more you are listened to and the more you get to control your message.

What is your code of ethics?

Does your communications team have a code of ethics that details the standards they must uphold?

In Australia, journalists are bound by the Media, Entertainment and Arts Alliance Code of Ethics. The code states journalists are committed to "honesty, fairness, independence and respect for the rights of others". In a DIY Newsroom, staff might more appropriately be covered under the Public Relations Institute of Australia code. It tells members they cannot "knowingly disseminate false or misleading information ...".

You could develop your own code to reflect your company's culture and aspirations for staff. I encourage you to endorse some form of charter so employees know which way your organisation's moral compass points.

To kick off the conversation, consider this six-point code:

The DIY Journalist Code of Ethics

1. Tell the truth, the whole truth and nothing but the truth. Do not lie, embellish, sugar coat or dodge the truth by omission. Nothing good comes from any of that.

2. Serve your audience by providing them with useful and engaging information.

3. Do not waste people's time.

4. Say something when you have something to say. Otherwise don't. Never spam.

5. Be interesting.

6. Be professional.

What would you add?

CHAPTER 19

RESULTS

*"If you can't read the scoreboard, you don't know
the score. If you don't know the score, you can't tell the
winners from the losers."*

BUSINESS AND INVESTMENT GURU WARREN BUFFETT

Show me the money!

Let me share with you some examples of the types of situations
I regularly experience:

- I'm sitting in an airport lounge. Opposite me is a businessman
  having an animated conversation. "I am not going to approve
  that, Pete," he says. "Not unless I know the money we spend
  will be returned straight to the bottom line."

- I'm in my home town having a coffee with an executive. "We
  are doing plenty of social, Stuart, but I'm not convinced we are
  getting a return for all this activity," he says.

- Ping. I'm reading an email from a business leader. There is no
  point "fishing for any fish", he writes. "What I really want is to
  have a small number of wanted/desired fish … those which give
  us market leadership and dominance."

- I'm sitting in a management meeting in a city newsroom. "Only 10 per cent of the stories we do online resonate with our audiences," says the editor. "We are doing too much volume for not enough reward. Why?"

Targets. Results. The *right* results.

Today, an entire industry has emerged around ROI (return on investment) across every business activity. Content marketing is a booming multi-billion-dollar global industry, but increasingly CEOs and CFOs are putting the screws on their marketing people. They want to know, what is all this activity *worth*? What is the point of building audiences through blogging, tweeting, posting and uploading? What does this bring to the bottom line?

It reminds me of one of my favourite pieces of movie dialogue. Cuba Gooding Jr's character Rod Tidwell is giving Tom Cruise's Jerry Maguire a hard time because Rod's dream NFL deal has not transpired. You know the scene? Tidwell is in the kitchen at his home while Maguire is sweating it out in his office in the unforgiving corporate world. Tidwell wants Jerry to show him the money, and has him say repeatedly, with increasing volume, "Show me the money!", "*Show me the money!*"

We all want results.

Deciding on the metrics that really matter

Results must be at the heart of all communications activity in a DIY Newsroom. Those results may be about the money, or how communications provide a pipeline to that money; for instance, an email newsletter with a call to action (CTA) that results in an inquiry that leads to a conversation that results in a contract for work.

But there may also be other drivers behind the metrics, depending on your organisation's central objectives; for example, non-profits clearly have a different reason for being. You need to decide on the right metrics for your organisation.

But how?

It can be as simple as this:

1. Get the right people in the room.
2. Brainstorm by mind mapping all possible benchmarks.
3. Revisit the company's strategic mission and objectives.
4. Check that the company strategy aligns to your communications strategy.
5. Settle on a dozen benchmarks that serve your business and communications strategies.
6. Cut the number in half.
7. Discuss, consult, review, confirm, communicate.

If all you come away with from this is social media metrics – such as "likes" or "shares" – you need to broaden the thinking. The number of likes on your Facebook page and web visits may well figure, but they only tell part of the story.

Other metrics might relate to:

- productivity of your team; for example, number of posts, campaigns, blogs they create each month
- calls to action that you make, and the number you convert; for example, opens on CTAs in email newsletters and any inquiries or sales that follow
- events you stage
- networking appointments or number of pitches made
- media mentions.

When establishing metrics, consider if they are:

- **Aligned to real value:** Make each metric as quantifiable as possible. Show me the money, or at least the link to another tangible outcome.
- **Relevant and fair:** Be realistic about what is within the remit and influence of your communications team. Do not judge staff on direct sales if that is not their role.
- **Minimal:** Six? You may even want fewer metrics to focus on. Or change a couple each quarter to bring new activities into the spotlight.
- **Goal driven:** The purpose of benchmarking is not merely to audit business performance – it is about matching metrics to achievable targets. A stretch goal is good, but do not make it an impossible climb.
- **People driven:** Metrics provide a great reference tool for evaluating performance. In themselves they can be used for employees' KPIs.

As an example, here are five relevant metrics you might want to track:

1. number of sign-ups for your main newsletter
2. number of likes on your Facebook page
3. total reach for top five posts/communication activities for the month
4. number of client inquiries from communications activities for the month
5. number of external presentations for communications staff for the month.

Get the above right and metrics will provide you with a clear line of sight – from your headline objectives through to performance.

Gathering the data

Social and digital platforms carry informative data and analytics, but you will also need to draw on other information and processes to provide greater context. For example, this could include tapping into internal company reports for data on sales inquiries emanating from your marketing activities.

How should this be done and who should do this? Ideally, in the DIY Newsroom communications and marketing staff should determine and manage metrics.

Social media management tools such as Hootsuite and Buffer can aggregate some of this information. Other services can provide aesthetically beautiful reports. However, the best result is if you can bring this information together into a dashboard for all to see.

For that, options include:

- **Off-the-shelf digital tools,** which may require further customisation to ingest data.
- **Building or customising a tool yourself.** Can your IT department do that simply, cheaply and quickly?
- **Going old school.** Make it someone's job to drag the data into a spreadsheet and update it manually.

I have seen approaches that are spectacularly unsophisticated but still eminently practical. In one newsroom, a whiteboard that listed traffic goals and performance (very wonkily drawn, I might add) sat pride of place. Perfectly practical.

Sharing the data

Whatever you decide, the information you gather needs to be shared. Hey, you're in the communications business, remember. Distribute results to your people, to other stakeholders in the business and – where relevant – externally, say to trade media.

When I was national editorial director, I would send a monthly summary of digital results to our 800-plus staff. This detailed overall results, growth against previous months, and state-by-state results. I provided top 10 lists and a link to spreadsheets carrying the complete breakdown. That "show and tell" fuelled rapid digital expansion by celebrating successes and fostering a competitive environment.

Manage up too. What does the CEO want to know? Because their time is precious, a one-page monthly summary may be apt. Even better, provide your CEO with a graphic of your dashboard – complete with the dials you are moving, and a bar graph of increased sign-ups and the like.

In communicating about your communications, make it visual, simple and aligned to the ROI pipeline.

Seeing is believing

I often tell the story of the newsroom where we piloted a national digital transformation program. This newsroom was bordering on the moribund, but that changed when we started displaying the team's digital analytics on a $300 TV monitor. I watched a reporter literally jumping up and down as she saw the number of people who were reading her story online at the time. The editor also began spending more time in the body of the newsroom. He was mesmerised by what he saw on screen.

The lesson? Seeing is believing.

Analysing and improving

The Results part of the SMART Way is not just about recording and reporting. It is also about interpreting and leveraging those results to improve performance. Data in itself serves no purpose unless it is analysed, contextualised and used for continual improvement.

Hold regular strategic reviews, quarterly or more often, to ensure everyone is on message and on song. Use the information you have gathered in a constructive way at weekly meetings, to make sure next week is better than this week.

The dangers of metrics

If not used well there can be some downsides to metrics. Here are some risks to look out for:

- **Don't divorce the data**: If IT, product or other departments are collecting the data that matters to you, ensure you have routine access. The best newsrooms put data at the centre of what they do.
- **Avoid paralysis by analysis:** You can be quickly overwhelmed by a tsunami of numbers. Keep your tracking simple, relevant and in context.
- **Don't become a robot**: Big data and artificial intelligence are changing the way we work. But rage against the machine. The best businesses will continue to be driven by superb human decision making.
- **Don't believe everything you read:** Is your data correct? In 2016, Facebook was forced to apologise because it exaggerated numbers of video views. Check and recheck the veracity of surveys, research and statistics. I have been caught out by numbers that were not correct or did not tell the whole story.

Revenge of the nerds: tools and tech

"If you're going to survive in the media landscape you need to have a holistic skills set and we all need to become 'Robocop' journalists where you have a big array of weapons at your disposal – drone in one hand, Facebook Live in the other."

MOBILE JOURNALIST YUSUF OMAR, SPEAKING TO *JAMLAB*

In itself, technology is meaningless. It is the results it enables that really matter.

Take the poster child of disruption: Uber. People were sick of paying exorbitant prices for a simple taxi ride in big cities, the inefficiency of the payment system, and the lack of visibility on when a car might arrive. Facilitated by a simple app and GPS technology, Uber solved those problems. The problems were real human ones. Technology delivered a better way.

Lots of solutions have been designed for communications. As I have already said, one of the reasons newsrooms are a great model for modern marketing is they are early adopters of technology. However, we are right to be cautious about what we introduce to our businesses and how any technology works with the other systems we have in place. I've seen companies where their technology ecosystem more resembled a 1950s telephone exchange than a slick, seamless, modern operation.

Developing a technology strategy

Organisations should develop a technology strategy. Your comms team will want to be front and centre in the discussion because technology is production critical for a DIY Newsroom. This is as relevant whether you are a small operation or a multi-national entity.

Those running a DIY Newsroom do not have to be technologists, but they do need to know the right questions to ask about technology and how any advancements could benefit or hinder the organisation.

A technology strategy would consider:

- **Integration:** Can your systems be streamlined? Are they sympathetic to each other? I use Google apps because of the ease of use, collaboration and connectivity.
- **Simplicity:** Less is more. Over time I have seen elaborate systems get overtaken more and more. Third parties can provide

many simple solutions that once upon a time required Hoover Dam–scale construction.

- **Specificity:** This is about what gadgetry, hardware and software is required. This can be uncovered in the communications health check (see chapter 16).

- **Business alignment:** Does new technology ultimately serve business objectives? Will it improve the customer experience, be it internal or external?

- **Cost minimisation:** The build or buy question. Do not let the technology monster gobble your budget.

- **Quick pivoting:** Does the company have the IT framework to "dump and run" – to quickly abandon outdated systems and adopt new, more nimble ones?

Typically, IT departments love to resolve matters themselves. "Oh, we can do that," is a common refrain. But custom builds usually cost a bunch of money, take too much time (which allows competitors to whizz past), and cause lots of heartache. It can be more prudent to buy a ready-made solution.

Rise of the machines

Artificial intelligence and machine learning will eradicate the complexity of many existing processes we find ourselves wasting time on at the expense of core activities. For example, virtual reality and facial recognition mean we will be interacting differently, again.

Amy Webb, an American futurist and founder of the Future Today Institute, told a conference I attended that a fundamental social shift would occur as people began routinely talking or interacting with devices and machines rather than keyboarding. When you think about it, that action – one-on-one communication, albeit with a machine – is a more human process than what we do now; typing furiously on mini-keyboards, swiping across, up and down, logging in and out of applications, and similar.

Also, systems will move from "dumb", with a relatively low level of understanding of what we are trying to achieve, to "smart", where they are driven by a frighteningly accurate understanding of our personal and professional needs.

Folks, hold on.

What tech does a DIY Newsroom *really* need?

When you walk into a modern newsroom there is a palpable sense of digital sophistication: banks of monitors show satellite news services and the latest numbers from stock exchanges; everybody has a smartphone within reach; and different platforms help with the dissemination of information.

In your DIY Newsroom, you want to convey the impression of a modern, digital operation. You also want it to function as one.

You will know by now that a DIY Newsroom is as much a way of working as it is a physical environment. But you can have the latter too without the need for huge capital outlay. Even a home office can establish most of the attributes of any modern newsroom.

What then are the components you need to be on the cutting edge? Here are some of the essential tech parts to build a DIY Newsroom:

- **A happening space:** The world is shrinking, and most of it seems to be able to be captured on the screen of a mobile phone. But we still need a place to congregate – a space where teams can meet, brainstorm and bounce ideas around. Your global headquarters does not have to resemble Apple Park in Silicon Valley. It could be a small corner of an open landscape office with daily morning meetings held at the local coffee shop.

- **A wired space:** Yes, there are places where there are still barriers to Wi-Fi and other connectivity.

- **The right hardware:** What devices should your business revolve around? Mobile, of course. The rest is debatable. I have seen different hardware mixes work in different circumstances. Some companies have gone in big for tablets. Laptops are essential for hot desking. In some newsrooms, I still see banks of PC monitors. I also usually see a range of new gadgets.

- **The right software:** Less is more. Integrated is great. Your technology strategy should aim to provide tools and applications that talk to each other, are cloud-based and easily collaborated upon. A common suite of office tools enables this. A strategy should start with an audit of what is used, and zero in on what is best practice. In a DIY Newsroom there are some quite specific needs for the gathering, management, editing and delivering of content. And what will you do for back ups, and video and image management and storage? Your health check (as part of your SMART Way) should surface any of those issues.

- **A social space:** Separately, you will want to consider social media management tools to make your life easier. You will want to consider those applications that can schedule social media posts and provide you with the best website and social analytics. Plenty of books and online resources will point you in the right direction.

- **A studio space:** You can get most of what you want for a studio cheaply over eBay or from a digital goods supplier. Even a small, well-equipped studio can set you up to produce video blogs, live stream to the web, and for other content. Add good lighting, microphones, a green screen and a presentable space and you are in the communications business big time. An alternative is to use an affiliate's or third party's resources – but ready access can become a hassle and a fixed cost.

Communication and marketing teams tend to outsource aspects of content gathering and production. This is especially the case around video, where hundreds if not thousands of dollars can be wasted hiring production teams to produce Hollywood-quality vision. Most of this you can do on a mobile phone and this will serve the bulk of your video needs.

Mobile journalism

Mobile journalism (mojo) should be central in every DIY Newsroom. It is the embodiment of do-it-yourself. In our personal lives we are constantly on our phones, but I do not believe we have unlocked mobile's full force yet. This is what mojo does.

Yusuf Omar, an international mojo celebrity, gave delegates at a conference I attended in New York a 20-minute tutorial on how easy it was to capture and distribute information with a smartphone. He called it "jeans journalism" because the tools he needed for storytelling – a mobile phone equipped with a handful of apps – fitted neatly into his pocket. The audience of mostly middle-aged media executives sitting in the TheTimesCenter, at the epicentre of global media at *The New York Times*, was fascinated by this exuberant young man as he walked them through how to effortlessly capture, produce and publish video storytelling, in this case to Snapchat or Facebook.

Mojo will become more mainstream, but already there are many resources to help you with this: books, Facebook pages and blogs, even conferences. One of the books that got me on my way is written by Australian journalist, trainer and lecturer Ivo Burum and Stephen Quinn (*MOJO: The Mobile Journalism Handbook*).

Mojo gives you five content superpowers:

1. **Spontaneity:** Mobile makes you quick. No need to book third-party agencies or to schedule videographers. Pick up your mobile backpack and get out there.

2. **Souped-up skills:** Most of your comms people are already tech-savvy. Mobile journalism should then be a walk-up start. Equip and encourage your team.

3. **Spark:** I have seen how one or two digital evangelists can ignite a movement in comms teams. Imagine what results mojo could bring to your communication and to your team.

4. **Synchronicity:** The world is mobile. Communications today are predominantly mobile. Thinking mobile, acting mobile, and creating content mobile to mobile will make your communications authentically ... mobile.

5. **Supremacy:** Combine mojo and a DIY Newsroom and you will create a remarkable competitive advantage.

A mojo approach should not be confused with an uncontrolled environment. Content delivered via mobile journalism still needs to be strategic and planned around your communications objectives. What it brings, though, is an entire new dimension of storytelling.

Commando mojo kit

Like the Jetsons, the futuristic cartoon characters who had jet packs, the mobile journalist is powered by a small backpack of gadgets. This might include:

1. **Smartphone:** With the maximum storage you can afford.

2. **Stabiliser bracket:** These can be hand-held selfie-style arrangements through to powered stabilisers or "gimbals" that make shaky videos look remarkably smooth.

3. **External microphone:** Depending on the assignment, you may want a direction mic or a lapel mic that connects to your smartphone. There is no shortage of choices at all prices, leading up to expensive TV-type radio transmitters. People will forgive ordinary video but not dodgy audio.

4. **Light:** Indoor video will usually need an additional light source. There are many affordable options.

5. **Tripod:** There are lots of small options for your phone and/or camera. A Gorilla Grip is a handy one too for your kitbag.

6. **Applications for shooting and producing:** Smartphone functionality and integration for producing and publishing video will become easier. In the meantime, apps are available that help users control exposure, light and similar, like a DSLR camera. Other apps help you edit and produce within the device.

7. **Wi-Fi:** If you plan to file from the field you will need access to public Wi-Fi. Or you can carry mobile Wi-Fi.

8. **Battery back up:** You need lots of juice for mojo. Plan for power reserves for your in-the-field work.

9. **Workflow:** With all this gear, you need to plot the quickest route to publish quality video content. This encompasses how best to upload and download media, housekeeping around clearing storage, and what you will use to publish. Mojo becomes part of your wider comms workflow.

Most of this gadgetry comes at a low cost, and more options are coming onto the market. Beware: compatibility of accessories keeps changing.

A DIY journalist can teach themselves most of what they need to become a true mobile reporter. But there are also low-cost training courses, from how to shoot video on a smartphone through to editing on desktop software.

Word of warning: mojo is extremely addictive.

The importance of reinforcement

"Mission accomplished."

BANNER IN THE BACKGROUND TO PRESIDENT
GEORGE W. BUSH'S SPEECH ON IRAQ HOSTILITIES ABOARD
THE *USS ABRAHAM LINCOLN*, MAY 2003

If you want to scuttle best-intentioned plans, do it like this:

- fail to document and communicate your vision
- be sloppy at planning
- put the wrong people in charge
- do not commit resources.

But the single most common failure I see, especially on transformation projects, is a lack of reinforcement and reviewing of progress. This means the good stuff does not get locked in and the bad stuff compromises the integrity of the achievements.

The reasons for this include:

- we feel we have won the war just by getting started
- we do not want to allocate any more time, energy or resources
- we have other hot spots to attend to
- we are bored with this stuff
- we feel time to reflect is an indulgence
- we believe near enough is good enough
- we have made the process changes and the rest is up to people to get on and do their jobs.

In the day-to-day battle of the workplace, these reasons can seem perfectly logical and acceptable. Unfortunately, they are poor excuses and will stunt the full potential of project outcomes.

On one big assignment I worked on I was disappointed not to get cut-through on my appeals for a project review. We had asked staff to adopt starkly new work practices. We provided them with training and new tools, and had done our best to communicate what we were trying to achieve. However, it was such a big piece of work there was bound to be slippage. Old habits re-emerged, compromise was allowed on work behaviours, and productivity did not meet expectations. Inevitably, managers began to ask what had gone wrong. One of the key issues was a lack of reinforcement about what was working.

Even before building your DIY Newsroom you should consider how best to review your work. A standard project management practice is to hold a "pre-mortem". Here, stakeholders can discuss and define what success will look like and what would scupper it. You can then mitigate those issues.

Committing to constant review is important too. Holding ourselves and what we do to account should be habitual, just like the behaviours we are trying to instil.

Forming great habits

Introducing new behaviours takes time. But how long?

I have heard 21 days mentioned. That figure comes from plastic surgeon Maxwell Maltz's observations in the 1950s of how long it took for a patient to become accustomed to their new face or to no longer sense a "phantom limb" after amputation.

However, a 2009 study from the University College London found it took people 66 days on average before a new behaviour became automatic. That period ranged from 18 days to 254 days depending on the person and circumstances.

What does that mean in a business setting? There is no absolute. But let us agree that embedding significant change takes longer than 21 days, requires active support and does not occur by osmosis.

CHAPTER 20

TEAM

"The deepest principle in human nature is the craving to be appreciated."

DALE CARNEGIE, *HOW TO WIN FRIENDS AND INFLUENCE PEOPLE*, 1936

Forming and organising your A-team

Communicating effectively today requires new thinking, processes and tools. It is in no small way why I developed the SMART Way and why I wrote this book.

But without organising and deploying your people wisely your success will be curtailed. Your people are the X-factor. Business leaders who recognise this, who create the right team culture, are the ones who will become the gold standard in their sector. You want to inspire your team, of course. Just as importantly, you need to organise them to make your new way of operating sustainable.

Starting with a clean slate

The first order of business is to form your A-team – and for this I suggest you take a clean-slate approach.

Do not think about who is on your team now. Put aside any initial hesitation because of HR complexities and existing job descriptions and personalities. Rip up your existing organisational chart. Instead, think in terms of what functions you require and how you would most logically arrange them. Do this from the ground up.

Ideally, make this a team exercise. The proviso would be that attendees have the capacity to think as objectively as they can without getting defensive about what change might mean for them.

My approach would be to:

- start with a blank sheet of paper or whiteboard
- list the main activities and tasks you require of your team
- refer to the other processes we have stepped out where relevant, particularly your media ecosystem
- group tasks and consider how they would comprise a specific job
- redraw your organisational chart.

You could group tasks under categories such as:

- content management
- content creation
- content production
- content distribution
- video and digital storytelling
- social media
- SEO and analytics.

You should be realistic about resources. That said, I have worked with department leaders who have successfully appealed to their managements for more resources because of this very process. If the powers-that-be see that improved communications will bring business growth, it follows that they should provide the resources for this to happen.

In the DIY Newsroom, it's accepted that most communication functions can be done from within. But in mapping your operational needs you might identify the need for external resource, such as for specialist services.

Having worked out your ideal team you can then consider how you go about any required restructuring. In my consultancy work and prior I have worked with businesses to help them do just this. In media and publishing, such work could result in quite dramatic restructures. From time to time, it has involved disestablishing entire departments and putting them back together to reflect the "future state". Many organisations do not have the stomach, or in fact need, to do this.

The flip side is that it's frustrating to see operations that would obviously benefit from recasting their teams just play at the edges. Meantime, those same managements complain about flagging results. In those circumstances, more duties and pressure fall on fewer staff.

The DIY news team

Here is what a DIY news team could look like. It does not take into account your circumstances, but it gives you a starting point for positions and responsibilities:

- **Editor-in-chief (*commander*):** Communications director. Strategist. Newsroom head-honcho. Leader. Sponsor. Audience advocate. Reports to CMO or CEO.
- **Head of content (*commander*):** News director. Operational leader. News commissioner. Coach. Editor. Trainer.
- **Head of visuals (*commando*):** Director of video, photography, graphics, presentation. Leads by example. Hands on.

- **Content creators/coordinators (front-line *comm*andos):** Storytellers. Producers. Across mix of media and chosen channels. Social. Print. Web. Cyber-journos. Mobile. Fully kitted.

- **Head of con-tech (*commando*):** Director of technology as it applies to content. Analytics. SEO. Reporting. Platform support. Trainer.

Organised for chaos

There is a wonderful scene in *The Paper* where chaos breaks out in the newsroom of a New York daily newspaper. The editor, played by Michael Keaton, is having various animated discussions. His star reporter is stretched out on the couch nursing a hangover. The news editor is hassling, ready to conference. The editor's ex-wife storms in. And a gun appears.

For those of us with newsroom experience, it is entirely relatable … well, maybe not the gun. However, you would be mistaken if you thought newsrooms did not have a structured way of working; that they ran on adrenalin and a whim. In fact, newsrooms are excellent at workflow. They are organised for chaos, so when breaking news occurs they can act quickly and expertly.

The attention to detail in regard to newsroom workflows has only increased in recent times as they have become leaner and more nimble operations. They are supporting – research shows – an extra six or seven communication channels. This has led to innovative solutions. In the best modern newsrooms, journalists can work on a story in one content management system but it is published across multiple channels: print, online, social and apps, for instance.

Embedding your new way of working

The ancient Romans regarded repetition as the mother of all learning – and workflow is the bedrock on which habits are formed.

In ushering in any new approach, such as the DIY Newsroom, staff may feel overwhelmed or anxious about the expectations on them.

However, combined with succinct job descriptions, the workflow you set out for your team should give them certainty.

Without a well-defined workflow, your operations will be disorganised. Bringing clarity to the way you want people to work is essential to making a DIY Newsroom sustainable. The best way to do that is with a no-nonsense audit and review of how you work now. After deconstructing this, you can put it back together to create the perfect workflow for your new way of doing things.

Here is how you could do that:

- **Gather who you need.** Your thinkers, your managers and the people who will make this work. *Comm*anders and *comm*andos.
- **Call for pizza**. We want this to be an informal, loose-thinking session.
- **Find a wall or whiteboard.** Raid the stationery and grab all the sticky notes you can find.
- **Stand.** And appoint a facilitator.
- **Brain-ageddon (Part 1).** Define activity areas or steps in the current content process and write these on individual sticky notes. Steps could include:
  - gather content
  - create content (written, video, audio)
  - enter content into CMS (content management system)
  - review content
  - approve content
  - publish content to Twitter, Facebook, Instagram, website and so on.
- **Brain-ageddon (Part 2).** Go a layer deeper. Using different colour sticky notes, break those steps down into sub-tasks.
- **Order.** Rearrange the activities and their sub-tasks in a logical, linear way.

- **Review and simplify.** What have you missed? Which tasks could be combined or eliminated to streamline the workflow? The object is to have fewer tasks for maximum efficiency gain.
- **Document.** Photograph your wall of workflow.
- **Consult, review and simplify further.** After the brainstorm, collaborate with others and further examine the workflow.
- **Communicate and trial.** Introduce and review as agreed. Make sure everyone knows about the new workflow.

When your A-team is in place and your workflow is lean and easy to understand, it's time for a little magic.

Inspiring your A-team

> *"Clients do not come first. Employees come first.*
> *If you take care of your employees, they will take care of the clients."*

VIRGIN FOUNDER AND BOSS SIR RICHARD BRANSON

If you work in the corporate world you probably understand how it often resembles a battle zone. According to the experts, the business environment is getting tougher. In his book *Office Politics*, Oliver James, the best-selling author of *Affluenza*, gives a burning insight into how the "dark triad" of personalities – Psychopaths, Machiavels and Narcissists – hijack our offices. James cites research that shows American society has become more competitive and more materialistic, and that this has fuelled more prevalent Machiavellian behaviour in today's corporate culture. A study showed senior American executives were four times more likely than the general population to be "subclinical psychopaths". Think Gordon Gekko from *Wall Street*.

As the boss, it can seem easier to run a "command and control" environment than a "trust and track" one. The latter requires more emotional intelligence, and not every boss sees the value in working one-to-one with their teams. Some prefer to keep their eyes firmly focused on the bottom line. But research shows that the best performing workplaces are ones that work together on a shared and inspired vision, not where fear rules. While some managers might get their kicks from a combative corporate environment, most people prefer a collaborative workplace. This does not mean everyone needs to be "people people". Some workers prefer to keep to themselves and make a contribution to the business in an unassuming fashion. They do not want attention.

In a piece for *Harvard Business Review*, Daniel Goleman, an expert on leadership development, said many managers mistakenly led only as a function of their personality rather than by strategic choice. The best leaders, he argued, flexed between six main styles: coercive, authoritative, affiliative, democratic, pacesetting and coaching.

I have worked for and with companies across the spectrum. I have worked in highly competitive and ruthless environments, and in more collegial atmospheres. As a consultant, I now get to choose who I work with, and it is more pleasant working with executives who build positive cultures.

Such workplaces do not have to pull their punches. They can still be aggressive in their ambition for better results, but they typically expunge three office negatives:

- **Fear.** About change. About doing the wrong thing. About whether staff can do what is expected of them.
- **Ego.** Where personal agendas override team harmony.
- **Toxicity.** Where staff are working to survive, not thrive.

Disrupt or perish

When I ran the regional newsroom operations for Fairfax (180 newspapers and associated websites), I designed a digital transformation strategy that required 50 staff from across Australia to report to a dedicated digital unit rather than their own newsrooms. This team was responsible for evangelising the transition to more digitally delivered content and was aimed at breaking the nexus around print.

Encouraging and cajoling had not worked, hence the disruptive approach of shuffling staff around and changing reporting lines. The kickback was huge, but the results were stunning and immediate. Digital traffic trebled across the network, a new digital culture emerged, and, in time, we devolved the team back to the management of local newsrooms.

The lesson? There is a time and place for evolution. There is a time and place for revolution.

Five essentials of creating a great comms team

Creating the right ambience in your workplace makes a difference to people's lives, professionally and personally. Introducing Swiss balls, office greenery and flexible working conditions do not in themselves constitute a culture. We have seen, for instance, quite a few Silicon Valley and other start-ups afflicted by cultures as sick as we see anywhere.

I like to describe an effective modern workplace's attributes via five Cs:

1. captaincy
2. camaraderie
3. celebration
4. communication
5. coaching.

Let's have a look.

Captaincy

Great teams have great captains. These leaders flex to people and situations. Such adaptability is rare, and often there are leaders for certain times. Winston Churchill was magnificent in leading his empire to victory. Post war, he was polarising and ineffective as Prime Minister. Not all leaders have to be bold, brash or even charismatic. Some of the best have a quiet, measured way of working.

Camaraderie

Or call it collaboration. For this, it helps to set out ground rules or values. Even our kids' schools do that today so everyone knows the expectations. Respecting each other's views means people do not feel threatened sharing their ideas or challenges. What sort of creed could your team develop to encourage team play and camaraderie?

Celebration

You have a job. You get paid – that is your reward. That is the view of some Ebenezer Scrooge bosses (yep, the ones who get the bonuses). But good leadership makes celebrating wins, even small ones, routine. A simple "thank you" works wonders. On bigger projects, think more creatively. Acknowledging an employee's achievements does not have to cost big money. Treat employees and their families with a night out. Give someone a day off or arrange a fun team excursion.

Communication

Lots of companies pride themselves on their external communications, but fail to tell their story internally and struggle to maintain motivation. Does everyone know the company position? When significant change is made, do customer-facing staff know the script? Staff surveys can show upper management to be highly engaged but the corporate vision falls away dramatically outside of company headquarters. Effective leaders are those who communicate regularly, with integrity and directly.

Coaching

Staff new to an organisation or an industry require more hands-on training and skill development than other staff. Experienced staff need stretch goals. And it does not matter what sector you are in, we all benefit from continuous learning. Unfortunately, some leaders think that once they employ someone they can put them on autopilot.

The CEO's role is to support and nurture their team. Their reports in turn do it with their departments, and so on. How is coaching embedded in your team? Employees can get frustrated and disappointed if their skills are not extended through training opportunities. You may not be able to give someone a pay rise, but can you send them to a conference or support them to gain new credentials? For their part, individuals can also take greater responsibility for self-improvement and self-learning.

People: your X-factor

Attention to team is the fifth step, and the last step, in the SMART Way. In practice it is the thread that keeps everything you do together. Your team is what gives your organisation and your communication its personality. Your success stems from how you form, manage and lead your team. As such, there is no more important aspect in developing an effective DIY Newsroom.

PART VI

NOW WE ARE HERE

CHAPTER 21

SIGNS OF SUCCESS

"Here's to the crazy ones. The misfits. The rebels.
The troublemakers. The round pegs in the square holes.
The ones who see things differently."

STEVE JOBS, APPLE ADVERTISEMENT

The benefits to your company

When you and your organisation have understood and started implementing a SMART-run operation, your communication operations will transform in at least seven ways:

1. You will have a strategic blueprint for extracting maximum value from your communications team.

2. You will achieve your goals for little to no extra cost.

3. You will consistently deliver compelling, relevant and high-quality content to the right audiences, at the right time and with the right media.

4. You will have easy-to-use and practical tools and processes for everyday operations.

5. You will have the capacity to adapt as required to the changing media environment.

6. You will be better placed to weather the bad times, be it trading conditions or a scandal, because of the goodwill your newsroom has generated.

7. You will not compete. You will not follow. You will lead.

DIY not only saves you money by ensuring what you spend on communications is targeted at initiatives with clear goals, it will create leads and generate revenue. Best of all, DIY saves you the most valuable resource you have: time. With a DIY Newsroom, you now have clear direction.

How long will it take?

So how long will this take to set up and implement? This depends on:

- the size of your organisation
- the resources you can draw upon
- the degree of difficulty of your communication objectives
- the skills and mindset of your people.

For a medium-sized organisation of 50-plus employees, for instance, you should be able to plan out your communications and hit the ground running within a few months, or even weeks. For larger organisations it may take a little longer. In many ways, this is for you to determine and make happen.

Signs of encouragement

Sometimes teams spin their wheels when they seek to move forward, and teams frustrated by their apparent lack of progress can fail to see how far they have actually come. When this happens, I tell them to look in the rear-view mirror to see where they were, and also to look for the signs of progress they may not have noticed. If a team is clicking, if it is powering at the right speed and in the right direction, there are tell-tale signs, even if the ultimate goals haven't been reached yet. In the early stages of building a DIY Newsroom you can expect to see:

- **Team exuberance:** People with purpose exude confidence about what they are doing. With a method in place, they start to see outcomes and this creates a new mood.

- **Calm amid crisis:** The world never goes to plan. But if you have one – a plan – you are grounded, and this is evident for all to see when crisis breaks out. When the comms team has it under control, the boss feels better and audiences get useful information, not reactive statements. The next day, people say, "Gee, they handled that well".

- **Curiosity about what you're doing:** Many industries have formal and informal networks and cliques. There becomes a certain prescribed way of going about business – and the sector runs as a herd. When you break away from the pack and get great results, this rattles cages and your competitors will want to know what your secret recipe is. They will do that by stalking you across social media. Expect direct questioning too, and other signs people are trying to figure out what you're doing right.

- **Momentum:** Things start to happen more quickly and unexpectedly. Campaigns that once were dull and languid receive sign-ups and results. Interest surges. The (nice) problem becomes how to handle the knock-on effects of better comms.

These are not hollow aspirations, as those who have gone the DIY Newsroom way will testify. Let's now hear from three major corporations that have implemented this method with great success.

DIY NEWSROOM SUCCESS: ANZ *BLUENOTES*

After visiting Silicon Valley in 2011, the board of ANZ Bank, one of Australia's "big four", knew the status quo would not serve the bank well given the tsunami of disruption about to hit financial services. The bank committed itself to a program of transformation, including to strategically engage audiences through social media.

Previously, the bank relied on the business sections of traditional media to present its thought leadership, research and commentary. But audiences were fragmenting and the bank needed a new way to reach them.

One solution was to create *bluenotes*, "a publication of ANZ's newsroom, a forum for insights, opinion, research and news about the economy, financial services, investment and society, from within ANZ and outside".

Managing editor Andrew Cornell said *bluenotes* produced the kind of content that previously would have been published in the *Australian Financial Review* or broadcast on TV business programs. "We are marketing ANZ's insights into business, insights into economics," Cornell said.

bluenotes is run by a team of three: Cornell and two other content/digital experts, who produce video, podcasts, text and infographics. About two-thirds of content is ANZ-sourced and the other third is from external contributors.

The *bluenotes* ecosystem represents a best-practice DIY Newsroom – a mothership news website, a direct email newsletter to 8000 subscribers and tens of thousands of ANZ staff (who go on to share content), and targeted social media postings across LinkedIn and Twitter.

The real impact comes from *bluenotes* providing authoritative content to an audience of highly influential and economically astute business leaders across Australia, New Zealand and the Asia Pacific. *bluenotes* avoids any retail marketing or product push. Cornell said:

> bluenotes *is a daily online version of the bank's thought leadership. Essentially, we are a business class lounge audience. They are generally business people, customers, prospective customers, people in the industry and importantly, policy makers, regulators and academics.*

The ROI is judged by the usual traffic standards of online shares and engagement, but reaching the right audience and maintaining a high level of discourse is just as – if not more – important. Again, Cornell:

> *It is not a quantifiable measure, but a significant measure is the kind of feedback our executives get when they're out in the real world from people who say, "oh I read something in bluenotes" or "you know, I get your email and it's really good". That happens right up to the CEO level.*

DIY NEWSROOM SUCCESS: BUPA'S DIGITAL NEWSROOM

Australia's largest private health insurer, Bupa, runs a lifestyle channel and most recently set up a digital newsroom as part of a two-pronged content approach.

The Blueroom is the insurer's customer-facing website, which provides credible and authoritative health and lifestyle information, especially for its target market of young families. The site is a subtle but effective marketing tool to connect to non-customers searching online for ways to improve their health and that of their family.

The other component of its content approach is a digital newsroom, which Bupa set up in June 2017 to modernise its corporate public relations. Head of Media and Corporate Communications James Howe said Bupa, like ANZ, could no longer rely on a fragmented traditional media to promote its brand. It decided to cut out the middle man and control its message by setting up a separate media room and website.

The site began with simple contact information and latest announcements. Like many corporations, Bupa found the job of disseminating run-of-the-mill media releases cumbersome and becoming less effective. Fewer journalists and more churn in the industry meant organisations did not have the relationships they once did with traditional media exponents. A digital newsroom could channel information straight to audiences.

"Having that ownership and the ability to do it ourselves was fundamental," Howe said. "That then meant also having the processes and policies in place internally to make sure we could operate at that speed."

A new content management system allowed Bupa to more easily curate and distribute words, images and video. In true DIY Newsroom style, the company's media website is central but Bupa uses social media in a smart way to supercharge that content.

Media, influencers, those working in the government sector, other industry stakeholders and anyone interested in health issues then use this as a point of contact. They have immediate access to Bupa's opinion on the issues of the day, along with other relevant data and storytelling.

"We have two separate streams for specific purposes. Internally, we describe it that the Blueroom is like your lifestyle channel, and Bupa media, or the digital newsroom, is your news and current affairs," Howe said.

Shortly after, the Australian Federal Government announced the most significant reforms in private health insurance in 20 years, and the digital newsroom offered a great depth of content about this. This included a video interview with the head of health insurance, live news pages, and other content that was distributed across Facebook, Twitter and LinkedIn. The marketing team followed up the next day with an email newsletter to all members, with links back to the Bupa newsroom content.

Only a small team of four, including Howe, runs the newsroom, but it can rely on the wider resources of the organisation. The team includes an award-winning journalist and a former network television reporter.

I wondered how to best describe this hybrid corporate news offering. Was it content marketing? Did it constitute journalism? Or was it public relations on steroids?

Howe said:

> I think it is something new. It essentially becomes a tool to build
> a more meaningful relationship with your customer, or to engage
> with your customer in a different way. To keep having touchpoints
> with them, even at a time they're not spending money or not having
> to use our services. We want it to be actually something useful to
> the customer.

It makes economic sense too:

> If you're wanting to turn over the volume of content that we do, if we
> were outsourcing everything we would just go through the budget way
> too quick. By having that in-house control, we can actually set the
> pace, and turn things around quicker and cheaper. For us it works.

DIY NEWSROOM SUCCESS: AFL MEDIA

I have mentioned the AFL elsewhere, but it would be remiss not to include
them here when talking about gold-standard newsrooms.

In a short seven years, AFL Media has positioned itself as part of, well,
the AFL media. For those of us with roots in traditional media, it was
not too long ago that anything that faintly smelt of PR had no chance of
legitimacy in the eyes of the journalistic fraternity, let alone information
provided by a self-interested party. Today, AFL Media journalists sit
alongside Melbourne's finest sports reporters at media conferences and
ask questions. As well, AFL Media and other communication staff from
other sectors are welcomed to industry forums and groups such as the
Melbourne Press Club.

The lines between "journalism" and "corporate communications" are
becoming blurred. This is not without issues, certainly around the
distinction between truly independent journalism and everything else.
But as *bluenotes* managing editor Andrew Cornell pointed out, audiences
today want to know their information can be trusted – which does not
mean it cannot come from a variety of sources, including those involved in
the sector.

The particularly exciting aspect of AFL Media's success is that, having gotten all the communication fundamentals right, the unit is positioned to positively shape the future of the game. In the AFL's case, controlling its communications is helping the sport extend its territory to other non-AFL constituencies, increase female participation and the female fan base, and to influence the new migrant population. AFL Media now has that sort of extended firing range.

CHAPTER 22

WHAT'S IN IT FOR ME?

*"With realisation of one's own potential
and self-confidence in one's ability,
one can build a better world."*

DALAI LAMA

You.inc

Now I want to get personal. I want to talk about *you*. Whether you are running the business or play a role in it, what is in it for you to create this change in your organisation?

CEOs and their executives are incentivised around various KPIs. Businesses have more rounded ethoses today, and not everything is about profit. But often what people yearn for most, despite it not always being overt, is recognition for the work they do. This is not unhealthy egotism. And modern communications provides an unprecedented opportunity for professionals across all fields to propagate their knowledge for greater public good.

This WIIFM (what's in it for me) is strong for both *comm*anders (bosses) and *comm*andos (those in the trenches). And I make you this promise: when a DIY Newsroom is functioning as I describe it, this will change the way *your business* is seen and it will change the way *you* are seen.

This is enthralling to watch as individuals and their companies grow in tandem. When that happens, the people at the centre of it become recognised as industry leaders, they are feted, and this propels careers. They become influencers, thought leaders and authorities in their area. For careers to boom, there is nothing more powerful than recognition.

With a successful DIY Newsroom in place, you can expect to be:

- asked to speak at local, national and international conferences
- visited by parties who want to learn from the best
- promoted in your organisation and headhunted by others
- called on stage to accept awards for your organisation's work
- sought to contribute to industry journals, symposiums and the like

- seen as a trusted subject matter expert – even as "the authority" in your area
- encouraged to teach others how you did what you did
- approached by new talent who want to work for you.

This, and much more. In short, you will receive the kudos for the hard work you do. And why shouldn't you?

Your personal DIY program

The principles and practices that drive a DIY Newsroom can be applied in a strategic fashion to an individual's communications framework. A clear benefit is helping executives and their team members to prioritise their energies and to flex the right muscles – the same as with personal fitness training.

Acting authentically is critical, not the least for how a business leader uses social media. The Sirens of social media are ever present, and many leaders easily lose focus, or worse, because of ill-thought posts. Reputations built on social media can in the blink of a tweet be destroyed.

But individuals can establish a strong personal brand by using precisely the same SMART Way and principles.

CHAPTER 23

WHAT'S NEXT?

"Exploration by real people inspires us."

PHYSICIST STEPHEN HAWKING

Value of the human touch

Artificial intelligence and other technologies are bound to have a huge influence in our lives. In communications, we may see a whole new level of reach possible.

I doubt, though, we will lose the human touch. The bigger our world gets and the more access we have to every corner of it, the more we seek belonging, human connection and community. The greater the volume of information we must process, the more we want this to be filtered and the more we realise that a simple life is a good life.

If change is going to happen faster, as everyone says, then the human dimension will become starker and more valued. I'm even wondering whether we will see a sharp turn, a back-to-basics revolution, marked by the following:

- **Turn on, tune in and drop out of social media:** In some countries, Facebook is reaching saturation point and is an established mainstream media. Having lost its shininess, we are now more questioning of its place in our lives. Will engagement levels drop? Probably. Maybe there will even be a rebellion, a '60s-like turn on, tune in and drop out of social media. If that were to happen, I would not be surprised if those who led the revolution were not the Gen Xers or baby boomers but the younger digital natives looking for more authentic, real experiences. Because, to them, that would be new.

- **Renaissance of bespoke:** Call it the human touch: handcrafted, quality goods and services. Think craft beer not the standard amber fluid in a can. Content that is beautifully and imaginatively created will surely be more prized. Already, large companies that once outsourced their customer service are reappraising the virtue of providing a personal experience.

- **DIY simplicity:** Content marketing has grown exponentially as a solution for businesses to help them create, curate and channel content. But a Sensis study found the bigger end of town was starting to spend less on digital marketing, dubious about the ROI. Businesses will still spend money on targeted campaigns, but DIY is just as economical, keeps control at home and provides a bunch of other benefits.

Coherence from disorder

When I was on a study tour in the United States in the late '90s, I spent time at the *Chicago Tribune* where Jack Fuller was president and publisher. Fuller had written a book, *News Values*, which 20 years later establishes him as a communications prophet.

In 1996, the internet was taking off but Facebook and Google did not exist. Newspapers were still enjoying double-digital growth, but you could see the signs of change. The MIT Media Lab was researching the Daily Me, the notion that technology would curate a digest of news and information for the consumer, delivering it to them electronically. It is what we see today – sort of.

Fuller questioned whether this could ever satisfy an audience's search for meaning and authenticity. Accepting that the new medium offered its own form of creating communities, Fuller nonetheless argued there was something special about newspapers. Newspapers had a sense of character, stood for something, gave context, led communities, and were people-driven. Where the internet could provide the Daily Me, newspapers had always been a kind of Daily We. And people, Fuller said, were looking for more coherence, not less:

People come to a newspaper craving a unifying human presence: the narrator in a piece of fiction, the guide who knows the way, or the colleague whose views one values. They want a synthesiser who can pull a world together from the fragments.

As we have seen, readers don't just want random snatches of information flying at them from out of the ether. They want information that hangs together, makes sense, has some degree of order to it. They want knowledge rather than just facts, perhaps even a little wisdom.

This is not a call to resurrect the place of the newspaper. Rather, it goes to reinforcing the power of communities in our lives. Merely producing a stack of communications is meaningless without a framework, an intent or community context. The communicator's role is exactly this, to build an enriching experience and to connect people through storytelling. We can do this via screens, but the impact has to be an utterly real one for audiences and to make a difference.

Don't forget this when you are developing your DIY Newsroom.

MY MESSAGE TO YOU

"Whether you think you can or
whether you think you can't, you're right."

AMERICAN INDUSTRIALIST HENRY FORD (1863–1947)

Your story. Your chance.

In writing this book, I wanted to provide business leaders with a manifesto – the case for a new approach. For those at the coalface, I wanted to give them a guide to the main components – a handbook for shaking up the status quo.

I wanted to help you find the coherence amid the chaos. I also wanted to inspire you a little.

Newsrooms and their journalism have been the catalyst for great things in our society. You can do the same. And if you believe in that, as a communicator you are in the most powerful place in your organisation. Because from your storytelling, ideas will be born, shared, and become reality.

The DIY Newsroom provides you with the opportunity to write your own story, control your message and make a tangible difference.

It is now over to you. The next chapter is yours.

FINALLY

You can work with Stuart

Stuart Howie runs a communications consultancy, Flame Tree Media, which helps clients implement the five-step SMART Way™. Flame Tree's services include:

DIY Newsroom™ transformation program

One-on-one support and guidance that gives you the tools and confidence to establish what you have just read. It puts you on the launch pad for more effective communications.

Discovery session

A starter workshop that helps organisations unpack their problems, shows them a better way and provides immediate insights and solutions.

The SMART Strategy

The complete diagnosis and tailored plan for renewed communications health.

Workshops

- **Strategy to Action:** Hands-on session to convert thinking to doing.
- *Comm*ando **Bootcamp**™: High-intensity training that teaches frontline staff how to deploy the weapons of mass communication.
- And a range of other sessions to meet your needs.

Consultancy

- Strategic planning
- Project management
- Subject matter expertise
- Social media strategy
- Crisis communications
- Corporate presentation work.

As well ...

- Subscribe to the Flame Tree News newsletter
- Read our blogs, watch our vlogs

Contact the author direct

stuart@flametreemedia.com.au
flametreemedia.com.au
flametreemedia.co.nz

INDEX